Ann Lewis

This anthology is dedicated to the memory of
Margot Tennyson
Quaker Pioneer in Interfaith Work

*Be patterns, be examples in all countries, places, islands, nations, wherever you come, that your carriage and life may preach among all sorts of people, and to them; then you will come to walk cheerfully over the world, answering that of God in every one.*

George Fox, 1656

# PATTERNS AND EXAMPLES

# Experiencing the Spirit of Other Faiths

A Quaker View

edited by

Peter Jarman and Eva Tucker

with a Foreword by Adam Curle

A Hampstead Interfaith Group Publication

William Sessions Limited, York, England

Other books in the series:
*The Pure Principle – Quakers and other Faith Traditions,*
Jim Pym (Sessions 2000).


© Hampstead Interfaith Group 2005


ISBN 1 85072 336 2


Cover photograph of Mait's Rest Gully, Victoria,
Australia, by courtesy of Jean and Mike Jenn.
© Jean and Mike Jenn


Funded by the John Waterson Bursary Fund in
memory of Joy Blanche.


Printed in 12 point Plantin Typeface
from Author's Disk
by Sessions of York
The Ebor Press
York, England

# Contents

|  | Page |
|---|---|
| Foreword: **Adam Curle** | vii |
| Prologue: **Peter Jarman** | xi |
| Quakers in a Pluralistic Religious Environment: **Andrew Clark** | 1 |
| Quaker Way, Buddhist Way: **Peter Jarman** | 17 |
| Working with Quakers and Buddhists: **John A. McConnell** | 29 |
| Flirting with the Buddha: **Jonathan Fryer** | 55 |
| Some Aspects of Islam: **Ihsan R. Rasmy** | 65 |
| Across the Indus – Bridges of Faith: **Jennifer Kavanagh** | 75 |
| Some Aspects of Hinduism: **Hallam Tennyson** | 87 |
| A Point of Light – Meeting the Brahma Kumaris: **David Cadman** | 95 |
| Searching for the Kingdom – A Tapestry: **Mary Cook** | 101 |
| A Goddess-Loving Quaker Ponders Her Dilemmas: **Alison Leonard** | 111 |
| Interfaith Influences on Spiritual Development: **Judy Moody-Stuart** | 125 |
| Some of My Best Friends……: **John Dunston** | 131 |
| Special Expressions – A Jewish Childhood: **Eva Tucker** | 141 |
| A Soul for Europe – Ethics and Spirituality: **Richard Seebohm** | 149 |
| Afterword: **Eva Tucker** | 155 |

# Foreword

## Adam Curle

I AM FASCINATED and impressed by the knowledge and wisdom shown by contributors in the presentation of their experience and understanding of the great variety of faiths shown on the pages that follow. Tolerance and sympathy would in any case be expected, but the depth and variety made me feel ashamed to be writing this introduction. I only agreed because my age and situation free me of the responsibilities of busier and more active Quakers – and because of the interest of the topic.

All the same, I thought that the request to me to write an introduction to this publication was a mistake, but a flattering one. And I have to say, after reading several of the contributors, that my reaction had been quite correct. This book is wise, stimulating and exceedingly interesting. Moreover, since I was asked only to write a few hundred words, I thought I couldn't do much harm.

My own first experience of another faith was as a student of twenty one living among Muslims in a village in Upper Egypt. The charitable generosity of the villagers was wonderful, and I was profoundly touched by the gentle devotion with which they responded to the Calls to Prayer – and their kindly thoughtfulness to me.

Many decades later I was again among Muslims – in Pakistan. Although the wider society was often explosively violent, I rediscovered the same amazingly friendly generosity, a core of gentle sweetness, as I had done in the Middle East.

My experience of Mahayana Buddhism was of a different kind. I first met the Dalai Lama at a distance, if I may put it like this, when he was addressing a large audience in Italy and was being translated into English by an Italian, a difficult feat for the poor man. As I listened, I realised that he made occasional mistakes. At the time I accepted this without question. Only later did I realize that the Dalai Lama's mind had somehow communicated with mine, not by words but by meaning, without an intermediary.

Some time later, my wife and I were dining in a restaurant in Bangkok. We were expecting the arrival of another Quaker who was coming from some distance away and we had no idea when he would arrive. Suddenly one of our friends, a very sensitive young Thai monk said, 'John will be here very soon, I'll just go and meet him'. He went out and in a couple of minutes returned with our other friend. The night was very dark and the position of the table would in any case have made it impossible for him to see anything outside.

Of course such examples of the extended mind are not necessarily proof of spirituality, they may well be demonstrations of intense training. However, in association with compassion, wisdom, loving kindness and generosity they contribute to the power and purity of all religious faith.

I would like to make some reference to African religion. Until recently, and perhaps sometimes still, this just meant to many people Christianity practised by Africans, but under the aegis of the former colonists. There is little realisation of specifically African religion beyond what are scathingly termed witch doctors. I know, however, of at least one institution in which Tibetan Buddhism and African spirituality are in close contact. Lamas have met with African spiritual leaders and both found themselves in considerable accord.

The specific reference to Buddhism brings me to a matter which I believe to be of considerable, but largely ignored, significance: the difference between national forms of the 'Religions of the Book', based on the existence of God, and

Buddhism, Daoism and other smaller related religions which are not.

Christianity, Islam and Judaism are, of course, notorious for their potential bellicosity. On the whole Buddhism and the comparable faiths are not. But how is it that Christianity, established on the wonderfully peaceful, wise and creative teachings of Jesus – the basis of Quaker faith and practice – should have been implicated in many more religious wars than the Buddhists and kindred faiths?

I leave my own speculations on this issue to wiser and more learned Quakers. It is perhaps one of the key issues for searching debate and action among those concerned with the issues raised in the following pages.

# Prologue

## Peter Jarman

*Love was the first motion, and then a concern arose to spend some time with the Indians, that I might feel and understand their life, and the Spirit they live in, if haply I might receive some instruction from them, or they be in any degree helped forward by following the leadings of Truth amongst them. And it pleased the Lord to make way for my going at a time when the troubles of war were increasing and when by reason of much wet weather travelling was more difficult than usual at that season, I looked upon it as a more favourable opportunity to season my mind, and bring me into a nearer sympathy with them. John Woolman, 1763.*

IF I CONSTRUE Indians in a modern context to be people of another faith tradition, then these humble words of John Woolman well describe the intention of contributors to this anthology.

Perceiving the ocean of another faith, whose waters have been fed by hidden springs of revelation from centuries of human consciousness, I might gingerly enter into its shallower waters. Or I might prefer to know about other faiths from those who have plumbed its depths. This anthology describes the experiences of those who have ventured beyond the shallows of another faith to experience a little of the power and beauty of its ocean depths.

There has been a substantial engagement between oriental and occidental faith communities for the first time in the twentieth century, and this anthology reveals ways in which its contributors have been affected by this encounter.

The hallmarks of this anthology are involvement, quickening and engagement in personal committed ways. However, the authors remain rooted within the Quaker faith community with the exception of Ihsan Rasmy, a Muslim, and John Dunston, a Jew: contributors have not become converted to another faith in any formal sense.

Some contributors make critical comments about the current faith and practice of British Quakers. For instance, the difficulties and dilemmas amongst Quakers in resolving their interpersonal conflicts. These are quite often allowed to rumble on to the detriment of the spiritual health and social life of their Meetings. John McConnell suggests that a Buddhist approach that identifies the root causes of conflicts and ways of transforming and healing interpersonal wounds would be beneficial to Quakers. Other contributors encourages Quakers to come to Meetings with hearts and minds properly prepared.

Whilst Buddhism and Judaism are having the most influence on Quakers today, there are accounts in this anthology of the influence of Islam, Hinduism and Brahma Kumaris.

The editors have been in contact with about forty potential contributors. We regret that eventually only fourteen were able to provide substantial essays: we asked initially for about 3000 words and we are grateful for those contributors who persisted despite substantial other commitments to complete this task.

Eva Tucker and I are members of the Quaker Committee on Christian and Interfaith Relations and we view this anthology as supportive of their work. We are indebted to the Hampstead Interfaith Group for sponsoring this publication with financial assistance from the John Waterson fund.

We much appreciate the support and practical help from Alec Davison.

# How does the Emerging Pluralistic Religious Environment Affect the Climate of Spirituality in which Modern Quakerism is Practised?

## Andrew Clark

IN 1960 I WON a travel scholarship to the Holy Land from a Quaker School, and from there my curiosity and adventures began. Over the ensuing four and a half decades I acquired in some measure the professional disciplines of relief, rural development, peace and international affairs and human rights which variously provided me with my livelihood. I lived in Nigeria, Bangladesh, Vietnam, Ethiopia but mostly in three Indian states, for periods varying between three months and eight years.

The personal observations below arise from a series of encounters with various world faith traditions, either meeting them or working with or for them. The check list of faith or belief traditions mostly gives vignettes of experience: what attracted me, what happened and what I learned. The purpose is to recognise the context from which my conclusions are drawn.

When I refer to others, usually former employers, whether Oxfam (1973-81), Friends Service Council, FSC (1968-70 and 1971/2) and Quaker Peace and Service, QPS (1982-99) or the International Association for Religious Freedom (IARF 2000-05), I am nevertheless writing strictly in my personal capacity.

**Bahá'ísm** I first encountered in that wonderful temple in Kampala, entering as a Methodist woman was softly singing, unaccompanied but with haunting echoes from the nine high arches: Morning has broken, like the first morning, blackbird has spoken, like the first bird.... Their integrity and suffering, particularly modern martyrdom in Iran, stir the deepest emotions of sympathy and empathy.

**Buddhism** is probably the favourite with Quakers, its use of silence, concern about suffering, vegetarianism and promotion of peace are seemingly natural points of synergy. I was sent by Oxfam to South Vietnam as a consultant for the Buddhist social action groups based primarily in the Vanh Hanh Buddhist University but also in the provinces and in Cambodia and Laos from 1973-75. Once I had a nonviolent bodyguard of Buddhist monks and nuns to escort me into a Communist-held area.

The monks and nuns created a teaching course for foreign NGO staff at our request. I was most astounded by the doctrine of *anatta* (no soul) which high lit for me an unrecognized problematic attachment of Christians to their souls. The monks cited Walpola Rahula's *What the Buddha Taught* [1] as the best introductory text for Western minds. When I subsequently met him together with Adam Curle in both London and Sri Lanka, a decade later, I was disappointed that he was not advocating nonviolence in response to the Tamil Tigers..... The problems which the hard line traditional Sri Lankan Buddhists posed by objecting to peace proposals and insisting on a privileged place for their faith community in the constitution, appeared to be a form of attachment to a political entity above its consequences in suffering.

I subsequently came to know two different modern Buddhist groups which had emerged in East Asia last century under venerable founders. They applied approaches to Buddhism which rapidly attracted a popular response, subsequently accumulating quite astonishing amounts of property and wealth for their institutions, while retaining Buddhist disciplines.

**Christianity** is my own tradition. Writing on Good Friday 2005, today would be the most important day in my religious calendar if early Quakers had not helped me to be wary of the dangers of holy days.[2] I have over the years attended most forms of Christian service or viewed their precincts, from the church with a temple format built by Dom Bede Griffiths in South India to the Orthodox onion domes of Moscow, from a palm-leaf roofed One True Church of God in S.E. Nigeria to the spires of Cologne Cathedral. My in-laws' Mennonite Church in the Canadian prairies is very like the Baptist church which I attended three times each Sunday in an English village. They are all responses to the life of the historical Jesus flawed or enhanced by the Church as a social institution which meets a wide variety of other, both valid and seriously questionable, human needs. Nor should Quakers escape a critical approach – but we can come to that later.

**Hinduism** Attending a ceremony sacrificing a chicken to the goddess of smallpox, Mariamma, made me feel very uneasy. I tried to show due reverence in all the right places but was I being co-opted or compromised? I am currently a failed vegetarian so, even in retrospect, I cannot object to the fate of the chicken. It is the idea that anything is achieved or purchased spiritually by the taking of life which is unacceptable, whether a chicken or a crucifixion.

That said, most of my early encounters with Hinduism introduced me to concepts with immense underlying wisdom and like reincarnation with important alternative ways of conceiving of the human condition. I would add briefly *Maya* (life as an illusion), *Ahimsa* (non-violence), *Appiagraha* (non-possessiveness) and the four *ashramas* (stages) of life, my having just entered the third (withdrawal from being the breadwinner!)

Hinduism has benefited from great reformers last century, such as Vivekananda and Mahatma Gandhi. Their religious teachings have been variously institutionalised in the Ramakrishna Mission and Gandhian ashrams, in one of which

I lived. ISKCON (the International Society for Krishna Consciousness, also known as Hare Krishna) claims to be a modern approach to more ancient Hindu origins, although it is regarded as a new religious movement (NRM), see below.

**Indigenous Peoples'** (Ips) **Faith Traditions** (sometimes called **Animism**) Standing by a Nigerian chief's door while he invoked the spirits, poured a libation of local palm wine on the ground and then invited us to sit down seemed quite natural, like 'saying grace'.

The ekpo (dancers dressed in raffia representing these spirits) were out on certain days of the year. (The colonial administrators had apparently insisted that they be licensed!) No women were allowed to be outside in these areas on those days. Since this would have grounded our Quaker medical relief clinics, our wise local chief decided that, when riding in a vehicle, nurses were "indoors".....

I subsequently attended a seminar for the leaders of all the local tribes and Muslim groups in an area of Mindanao (Philippines). The aim was to explore beliefs and religious freedom. We started with a religious ceremony, an invocation with incense by an old tribal leader which practically no one could understand because that language was almost extinct. When we came to discuss beliefs, even with translators, it was obvious that the Ips were nonplussed. The spirit world was the way it was, whoever would think of trying to explain it? (See also Shinto below). There was a fish god and a honey bee god, but nothing really hung together in a communicable theological system. It would be a mistake, however, to think that there was not one.

**Islam** The four Muslim group leaders at the same seminar had no such problem. They were completely versed in the teachings of Islam, and started explaining the Five Pillars without hesitation. As "people of the Book" Muslims expect Christians (and Jews) to know their scriptures and we lose their respect if we do not. The expectation that lay Christians would set aside five times each day for prayer does not occur.

Thus I am constantly impressed with the discipline of ordinary Muslims and for the respect which they show for Jesus as a prophet which is only rarely reciprocated for the Prophet Mohammed (PBUH).[3]

I was involved in writing to President Chirac on behalf of IARF on the issue of banning conspicuous religious dress or symbols in French schools. Muslims see their faith tradition not only for its revealed truth, but also as a bulwark against globalised decadence.

Much is cultural: I brought a Muslim visitor to my Quaker meeting on the Sunday that another Friend decided to bring his dog. Mercifully, Quakers draw the line at pigs and I saw the visitor show the same kind of bemused tolerance which had often been my lot.

Professor Abdullahi An-Na'im accepts that Islamic family law, practised in some forty Muslim majority countries.......clearly discriminates against women. Such communities equally, however, have communal demands for cultural self-determination. He argues for an internal discourse whereby Muslims can be persuaded to accept equality for women as consistent with their religious beliefs.[4]

**Jainism** Our family had Jain neighbours when I worked with a Jain colleague in Madhya Pradesh. Our baby daughter caused enormous commotion as she tottered towards their huge earthen water jar. Had she touched it, it would have had to be destroyed as polluted. Such was their perception of purity (and our lack of it), together with utter reverence for life, declining to eat any root vegetables since their extraction would disturb the insect life around them.

**Judaism** We kept the Ark of the Covenant in the corner of our Quaker Meeting House when the local Jewish community met there for many years. Judaism is in my experience a religion which acts as a bedrock for so many values. It is the one Abrahamic faith lacking an ambition to proselytise.

Edward Kemp's version of Gotthold Lessing's *Nathan the Wise* is an astonishing dramatic depiction of a Jewish leader in a multifaith conundrum in twelfth century Jerusalem.[5]

Being Jewish has become overwhelmed by its concomitant ethnic and geo-political identity. There are some brave organisations practising dialogue amidst the conflict, such as the Interfaith Encounter Association (IEA) in the Middle East. The director of IEA is a member of the IARF, a deeply devout man practising Judaism. He has succeeded in creating regular multifaith seminar-type gatherings across the faith traditions and promoting mutual listening and understanding about the applications of different faiths which actually highlight the absence of any intrinsic religiously based conflict.[6]

### New religious movements (NRMs): Cao Dai, Falun Gong, the Family, ISKCON, and Scientology

I met members of these movements which, with the exception of Cao Dai in Vietnam, have arisen since the middle of the last century. This is not the place to outline the peculiarity of their beliefs or practices, whether venerating Victor Hugo, chanting Hare Krishna in city centres, charging professional consultancy fees amounting to thousands of pounds to attain Clearness, a kind of spiritual keep fit exercise or (now discontinued) "flirty-fishing" to attract male recruits.

The new groups have, after the initial decades, modified some (but not all) of their more controversial aspects as public criticism has impacted upon them. They have matured and steadied down to focus on what is the central point of their message. This is probably what happened to Quakers as a process in the second half of the seventeenth century.

Two Falun Gong leaders visited my home and we were taken through the exercises. After our visitors had left, we mutually agreed to feeling significantly physically and mentally enhanced in a new and unexpected way. The Scientologists make bold claims to an effective methodology which breaks drug dependency amongst the young. I was most impressed with one ISKCON woman scholar who analysed a current issue of religious freedom and human rights law. Talking with such a group after a conference, they were able to recognise the problems their need to break away from their parents had caused – and yet to sustain the ultimate validity of the new spiritual path to which they were remaining faithful. In fact – far from being brainwashed – most people actually leave the so-called new religious cults to which they are attracted at a stage in their lives. A faithful minority remain convinced.[7]

The presence of NRMs tends to cause the less new religious movements most anxiety. This seems in part to be because – having achieved their own recognition and emerged from out of the stage when they were unacceptably new – they do not want to lose that hard-won credibility by being associated with the dubious newcomers.

Just because we were all new once there is, however, no need to hesitate to criticise beliefs or practices which seem prima facie dangerous or exploitative, as I shall argue below.

**Sikhism** The Sikh value of hospitality and social responsibility is very impressive. I attended a gurdwara in New Delhi which feeds about 2,000 people with a meal each midday, whoever comes. It is apparently a pre-condition for opening a gurdwara that one can give food to anyone who comes at midday. This would limit the number of Quaker meetings we could start quite drastically.....

**Shintoism** I was new to the kami, the immanent divine nature in both living beings and natural objects. The latter open ways to reverence for the whole earth which are also a deep part of Ips' worship. (see above).

In Japan, Shintoism (and Buddhism) are not perceived as religions. They are simply the way things are and always have been. Religions are new belief systems (like Christianity) which have been brought in and are to be regarded critically. However, ceremonial elements, like Christmas Eve worship or a Church wedding, may be assimilated according to the purpose they serve.

It was a bizarre moment for me when, after an important Shinto ceremony, the Priest's mobile phone rang. As he sought amongst his voluminous robes to locate it, the tune was unmistakably Bach's Jesu, Joy of Man's Desiring!

The Tsubaki Grand Shrine invited me to undertake the purification ceremony of misogi. This entailed stepping into a natural waterfall, suitably dressed in a white loin cloth and head band, after having completed various warm-up exercises, starting with *Furitama* (Soul Shaking.) The late *Guji* (High Priest) had done this every day, including deepest winter, for ten years as a process of supreme self-purification. Shrine (as distinct from State) Shinto sees itself as universalist.[8]

**Unitarian Universalists**, originating from Europe in the sixteenth century, are way ahead of the curve when it comes to the multifaith environment. Their rejection of a single creed is a common point with Quakerism, whereas their commitment to voting procedures in church government is a divergence. Like Quakers, the Unitarians have a distinguished line of forebears in science and industry from the Lunar Society (1765-1809) onwards.

The IARF was founded largely by Unitarians in 1900 with very considerable foresight, inspired by the 1893 World Parliament of Religions, and creating the first ongoing International Interfaith association. Unlike Quakers, Unitarians still suffer from rejection by the ecclesiastical establishment.

**Zoroastrianism** It is the practical strain under which ancient religions can find themselves in modern times which I came to appreciate. The traditional means of disposing of bodies after a Zoroastrian funeral is their consumption by vultures high on the Towers of Silence in Mumbai. The current severe shortage of vultures owing to a modern disease has led a modern Zoroastrian leader to devise solar panels to assist their disposal by focusing the sun to desiccate them.

*What have I learned in the light of this medley of experiences with people of other faiths?*

1. **That the ethos of interfaith is growing amorphously as a religious sub-culture:**

For a variety of historical reasons the modern interfaith movement marks the 1893 Parliament of World Religions as its beginning. Liberal Christians were however mostly preoccupied with the ecumenical movement for the first three quarters of the twentieth century. Just the last generation, aided by globalisation and the decline of commitment to membership of church denominations, has become significantly more curious about what other faiths have to offer. Article 18 of the Universal Declaration of Human Rights (1948) establishes Freedom of Religion or Belief. Minority faith groups in emerging multicultural societies have insisted on being heard. Diana Eck's Pluralism Project in USA seems to have surprised Americans to realise that they are the most extensive practising multifaith society outside India.[9]

The last quarter of the last century saw the resistance of the Establishments in many countries imperceptibly melt away. Religious leaders would stand on platforms together, receive each other respectfully and avoid denigrating each other's faiths. Public ceremonies would contain prayers by different faith leaders. Educational policy, except where secular, taught *about* the different faiths as a matter of academic responsibility.

The acceptance of interfaith as the prevailing global religious subculture is growing without any particular plan but as rational adjunct to the conduct of intra- and inter-community, and international, relations. Nowadays, it is unremarkable to find an interfaith council in any European or North American town or city, and there are equivalent national bodies. IARF is one of 14 international interfaith organisations.[10] Once again it leaves Quakers less on the cutting edge, another of our early tenets happily having graduated to acceptance by the mainstream.

However, there are still huge regions (not just pockets) of resistance, those for whom the clash of civilisations is a necessary stand. Nor does the emerging ethos necessarily run sufficiently deeply, as we shall see below. Some go along with, and to, interfaith gatherings secretly confident that all paths will culminate in theirs. It worries me when people are declared to be "Quakers but they don't know it", or "more Quakerly than most Quakers". We seem to want to pin our label on others without their permission.

## 2. That all paths are unlikely to lead to the top of the mountain:

I am indebted to my predecessor at IARF, Rev Dr Robert Traer, for his clarity of thought in response to the truisms that all religions are essentially the same or that they are different paths all leading to the top of the mountain. He points out that since we are ourselves on the mountain the analogy is not a good one. We are simply not in a position objectively to observe or assert where each path actually leads. We need to study our map, share it with others and relate respectfully to our fellow climbers, their maps, guides and any climbing associations to which we may choose to belong.[11]

Robert Traer's insight was to refocus the analogy from the properties of the mountain to the relationship between climbers. As I reflect on this, claims that a climber has come down from the top, or been divinely informed or transformed such that s/he certainly knows the right way, are implicit in many religious traditions. In my encounters with other faiths, it is a near certainty that some will mislead climbers who are striving for the highest. Bluntly, they appear to have aspects of being personality cults, exploitative and/or disrespectful of human rights. The climbers who are faithfully following these paths however are none the less worthy personally of our respect.

Indeed, arguably it is possible that all religious faith is neurophysically or psychologically induced in the brain as a part of its evolution. In which case all religions would be the same in the sense that none of them is true to its claims. The alternative is that, including within the process of constructive interfaith dialogue, we have to find ways to promote a meaningful Quest for Truth, the title of Robert Traer's book.

## 3. There is an increasing need for reform within faith traditions as a precursor for interfaith dialogue:

I can only see this quest starting from within faith traditions as it now does. It is by example that we have to advocate self-criticism. Ultimately interfaith dialogue could be an exchange of our self-critical processes, what we have learned from scriptural exegesis and how we have reinterpreted eternal truths.

IARF has recently produced a brochure *Towards an Affirmation of Religious Freedom and Responsibility*. [10] It is a relatively gentle encouragement to all faith communities to examine their own practices with a view to measuring performance against broadly held tenets of integrity, such as the universal Golden Rule and Islam's no compulsion in religion.[3]

The context is the United Nations (UDHR) Article 18 which establishes the right to hold, to practise and to manifest one's religion or belief. The Affirmation commensurately requires our ability to meet ethical criteria of responsible conduct which cover aspects such as: treatment of members (adults and children); changes of membership; public presentation; financial conduct; health practices and faith-based education. It currently omits the eventually much more controversial aspects such as religiously justified violence; the testing of conscience; self-mortification, self-immolation, extreme ascetic practices, séances, the use of illegal substances and ritual slaughter of animals.

**The effect of these three basic propositions applied to Quakerism** is easily minimised, but we do so at our peril. We need humility and awareness to guard our integrity and to start with ourselves. Quakers are expected to be open to the leadings of the Spirit and to have them tested in a mutually respectful but critically constructive process of spiritual discernment.

- Ensuring that we understand the religious terminology of other faith traditions before we embrace or use it. For example, Quaker silent worship is not, as is sometimes loosely alleged, like a sort of Buddhist meditation, with Quakers sitting palms up, eyes open only a crack, and thumbs touching. Buddhist monks are appalled at our inability to sit still, they are not expecting to be moved by the Holy Spirit to minister, and the process of emptying their minds while enhancing their consciousness is essential as an individual non-theistic discipline, not a process of centring down to a collective gathered meeting for worship.

- Sensitivity to the distinction between performance and worship. Quakers will support and attend interfaith services with a valid desire to enhance them and their progressive, liberal organisers' good intentions. There is however a point when we should be consulting how to ensure that, since we do not share the beliefs of the other religions, we are not spectators, leaving the others as performers. We are there because we want to understand, respect and relate to them. Thus, it is normally more appropriate for each community to explain the foundations and meaning of their faith and rituals, not to enact them in front of onlookers, however sympathetic.

- Consciousness that our openness and liberalism should not prevent us from engaging in disagreement. How then do we raise critical issues and face disagreement? Genuine interfaith dialogue admits of the possibility of imperfection in understanding one's own faith tradition or position. Take for example the different interpretations by Quakers of the programmed and unprogrammed, or the Christocentric and the Universalist traditions. The Friends World Committee for Consultation, FWCC, works quietly, even heroically, to keep the world family of Quakers in dialogue.

The element of imperfection and genuine mutual learning should be included, showing how we approach our own disagreements, and that they are not some kind of dirty washing to be hidden at all costs. Then I could feel able to engage respectfully but critically with another faith community, checking constantly that I had understood their underlying concepts. The key is the intention at an appropriate, but not too distant time, fully to engage by offering how we approach our own fallibility – and then listening to, and evolving dialogue around, what others identify as their strengths and weaknesses.

- Improving the discipline as well as ethical standards of putting our faith into practice. In this context too it would be both helpful and wise to begin to tighten up on our own spiritual sloppiness where it exists. We have quite enough integrity as the Religious Society of Friends not to feel insecure, or obsessively self-denigrating. Our problem areas are better identified by those Quakers at the forefront of the current debates about outreach or membership. The learning points are not so different and will have either echoes, or possibly antitheses, from those of other faith traditions.

## In conclusion

The emerging pluralistic religious environment affects the climate of spirituality in which modern Quakerism is practised with an enormous challenge. In olden days one Friend greeted another with: *How doth the Truth prosper with thee*

*Friend?* It is actually the word *how* which is the current challenge, and part of the answer appears to be to shift the interfaith paradigm into sharing our vulnerability and searching.

## References and Additional Reading

1. Rahula, Walpola (1990), What the Buddha Taught, Chapter 6.
2. Britain Yearly Meeting (1995), Quaker Faith and Practice, paragraph 27.42.
3. Zakaria, Rafiq (1991), Muhammad and the Koran PBUH = Peace be unto Him. Also Koran Surah II. 256 on p. 105.
4. An-Na'im, Abdullahi, The Synergy and Interdependence of Human Rights, Religion and Secularism in Runzo, Joseph et al. (2003), Human Rights and Responsibilities in the World Religions, pp.48 & 49.
5. Lessing, Gotthold, translated by Edward Kemp (2003), Nathan the Wise.
6. Interfaith Encounter Association: www.interfaithencounter.org
7. INFORM: Information Network Focus on Religious Movements: www.inform.ac/infmain.html
8. Yamamoto, Guji Yukitaka (1999), The Way of the Kami, p.82 and p.117ff.
9. Pluralism Project: www.pluralism.org
10. The International Association for Religious Freedom (IARF) 2, Market St., Oxford OX1 3ET. www.iarf.net/affirmation.
11. Traer, Robert (1999), The Quest for Truth: Critical Reflections on Interfaith Cooperation.

## The Author

Andrew Clark attended Leighton Park School and Birmingham and Manchester Universities. As a social scientist he specialised in rural development with a thesis on the social and educational impact of the Sarvodaya movement in 40 South Indian villages. He engaged in relief work for Friends Service Council in Nigeria (1968-70) and Bangladesh (1971-72). Working for Oxfam from 1973-81 he was seconded to the Buddhists in Vietnam (1973-75), and then he worked in Ethiopia and India. He was General Secretary of Quaker Peace and Service (1982-99), and of the International Association for Religious Freedom (2000-05). Currently struggling to finish building his house, manage a small woodland and improve at Chinese chess.

# Quaker Way, Buddhist Way

### Peter Jarman

IN MY EXPERIENCE I have been most inspired by the Quaker Way with its Christian roots and the Buddhist Way. Both Ways affirm the Sacred core of existence lying within and all around us. *Do not mistake my Way for the Other Shore*, advised Buddha: my *Way is a raft that can help you reach the Other Shore. My finger can point you to the Moon; it is not the Moon.* The writer of John's gospel attributes to Jesus the saying *I am (exclusively) the Way*, but Meister Eckhart re-interprets this saying (inclusively) as *Jesus said that I am Way*. Whilst I seek to be open to the breath of the Spirit from all faiths I do not choose to be exclusively a follower of one breath.

Living in Perth, Western Australia, in the mid-1960's, I stood weekly with George Appleton, the Archbishop of Western Australia, at the busy corner of two of the city's main thoroughfares to protest against the involvement of Australia in the Vietnam war including the conscription of young Australian males to fight there. At that time I read the account by a Vietnamese Zen Buddhist monk Thich Nath Hahn, *Lotus in the Sea of Fire*, that describes the witness of members of the Buddhist School of Youth for Social Service in attending to the suffering caused by that war. Two of his Buddhist associates immolated themselves in seas of fire in protest against the violence of both sides of that war. Buddhists were caught between the two antagonistic forces and suffered greatly as did all the peoples of Vietnam.

When twenty years later, I was appointed as the Europe Secretary of Quaker Peace and Service, Thay, as Nath Hahn is often referred to, came to small meetings of a dozen or so people at Friends House and the Quaker International Centre. I was struck by his peacefulness and simplicity, and his lack of anger about being exiled by governments in Vietnam from his home country. These small intimate meetings were held well before he became so well known and loved that he could fill the Central Methodist Hall. I regard myself as one of his many followers, and have a collection of his books at hand. Their titles serve as signposts on my way, including *Peace is Every Step, Touching Peace, Transformation and Healing, Living Buddha, Living Christ,* and *Going Home, Jesus and Buddha as Brothers.*

The action of Buddhists is directed towards the well being of all sentient beings. Thay has included the well being of the earth and its resources in an extended set of precepts, vows that Buddhist take.

My first encounter with Buddhism happened during my physics postgraduate years in the mid 1950's. I studied diverse philosophies and beliefs, including Daisetz Suzuki's's account of *Zen Buddhism* and Christmas Humphrey's *Introduction to Buddhism*. They quickened nothing in me for they seemed to be all too cerebral exercises not directed towards the relief of suffering, which I now recognise to be the hallmark of socially engaged Buddhism practised by Thay and his Buddhist community or *sangha* amongst others.

When Roswitha, to whom I am married, and I were appointed to be Quaker representatives in Moscow in 1991, I took Thay's biography of the Buddha, *Old Path, White Clouds,* with me and read a chapter a day in the bleak Soviet flat, our home for two and a half years. I also placed a large Russian Orthodox calendar on the door of our office and duly read the gospel readings ordained for each day, including most of Luke's gospel. The contrast between these readings was considerable: Thay's biography describes the natural miracles of mindfulness, awareness and compassion whereas

Luke's gospel includes many unnatural miracles apart from those of healing. What is more miraculous I believe is the transformation of relationships with one self and others to one of empathy in a spirit of love and truth. The gospel stories of Jesus feeding thousands by conjuring up food out of thin air would have been truly miraculous if Jesus had persuaded the crowd to share what food and drink they had. According to legend after Buddha died in his eighties from food poisoning, some of his followers sought to attribute unnatural miracles to him and even to make him into a God contrary to his teachings. Thay insists that miracles begin with our own self-transformation and lead to the alleviation of suffering.

Several unsuccessful attempts were made to kill Buddha by antagonists who felt that his life and teaching threatened their power and influence over others, and undermined their security. Such deluded people helped to crucify Jesus after only about three years of his ministry unlike the fifty or so years of Buddha's. Experientially I know that neither Buddha nor Jesus are dead: they are resurrected and are eternally present as the Inner Buddha, Amida, and the Inner Christ. As a Quaker what I recognise as the Inner Light is a manifestation of the eternal Amida and eternal Christ in whom we live and have our being.

I cannot accept the Christian doctrine of atonement, that Jesus by his death on a cross as a sacrificial lamb, reconciled us to God through his body and blood, and that through repentance before the breaking of bread and the drinking of wine in the Eucharist, our sins are washed away. I prefer the Buddhist view that we cause suffering through our ignorance and lack of skill, and that redemption lies not by any scapegoat spiriting away our guilt but by our awareness of the causes of suffering and our practice of the steps of healing transformation.

Whilst we were in Moscow, Thay led a mindfulness retreat that we attended. He also I believe sought advice from the official Vietnamese mission there about whether he and the Vietnamese Buddhist community living with him at Plum Village in France could return to their home country. Not until January 2005 was Thay able to visit Vietnam. He then with many members of the exiled community and friends were officially granted to meet freely with the Vietnamese people for the first time in fifty years and to have his books published there. Until this year they were banned as was Vietnam's United Buddhist Church. The faith and practice of some Buddhists appeared to be as threatening to the previous governments of Vietnam as was that of Quakers to the English establishment in the seventeenth century.

On returning to Britain, Roswitha and I participated in a retreat led by Thay at Gaunt House in Dorset. His long-term companion, the nun Sister Chan Khong, was with him there. Through sitting and walking meditation led by them, including a spellbinding meditation in a wood full of bluebells at which Sister Chan sang Vietnamese folk songs, and through Thay's Dharma talks, I felt led further along the Buddhist Way.

Two groups of socially engaged Buddhists were at that time meeting in London or nearby: the Fellowship of Interbeing and the Network of Socially Engaged Buddhists. The latter met in a home run by Catholic nuns in Southall, and meetings there were my first encounter with Christian religious practising Buddhist meditation. Subsequently I participated in Buddhist-Christian dialogues at the Buddhist Society, and similar dialogues organised by Elisabeth West at the Monastery of Christ the King in North London at which I listened to a dialogue between the Benedictine monk Laurence Freeman and the abbot of a Zen Buddhist community in California. They insisted that you cannot be both a Christian and a Buddhist: you need to be rooted in one or the other faith, but I feel that I can be both a Quaker and a Buddhist since neither has a strict creedal basis. It is not what you believe in that matters, it matters what you are. *What we are before God is what we are*, as Saint Francis remarked. Out of respect for Quaker ways, I have not taken any Buddhist precepts formally as is normal within a Buddhist community. However I have no difficulty in committing myself to their three refuges: refuge in the (inner) Buddha; refuge in the Dharma, the teachings of Buddha; and refuge in the Sangha, the community of people following in the steps of Buddha. Often I end a Quaker Meeting for Worship by saying within myself two graces: May the grace of the Lord Jesus Christ, the love of God and the fellowship of the Holy Spirit be with us now, and at all times. May the grace of the Lord Buddha, the love of the Dharma, and the fellowship of the Sangha, be with us now and at all times.

About ten years ago two therapists in Newcastle, Caroline and David Brazier, established the Amida Trust, an international Buddhist community based in Britain that is socially engaged. I appreciated David's first book on Zen Psychotherapy and was led to attend several day courses that they led near London. Later the hostess of these meetings invited me to mediate between the Amida Trustees and the officers and teachers of the Trust. I was at that time engaged in a modest way in bringing people together in war torn regions who had been alienated by violence, and felt that I could listen adequately to persons of the Amida Trust. As the Trust was a registered charity requiring a minimum of three trustees, and their numbers fell to two, I was invited to become one and I still serve the Amida Trust in this way.

At first I found that the sitting and walking meditation of the Amida community in their British centres and at their retreat centre in France was similar to Quaker practice if not too tight a distinction is made between meditation and worship. However this community has evolved distinctively into the Pure Land tradition originating in Japan. The core community now wears distinctive scarlet robes and has shaven heads. The rituals have become more complex with chanting particularly of the nembutsu, Amida Namo Bu, honour to the eternal Buddha. I do not yet feel at ease with this: actually I feel more at ease with the ritual of High Anglican services. I prefer a Quaker Buddhism without the ritual, robes and hierarchy of Buddhist orders. However I feel enlivened by the Dharma teaching of the Braziers, now Dharmavidya and Sister Prasada, through their books and courses. I especially appreciate Caroline Brazier's teaching and writings on Buddhist psychology.

The Pure Land within Buddhism does seem to me to have affinities with Quaker faith for its essence is that we cannot get to the Pure Land (= the Kingdom of Heaven) solely by our own resources. We need the assistance of the eternal Buddha (= the eternal Christ) to empower and enlighten each person.

There is a legend within Buddhism of a great Zen master catching up with a Pure Land devotee walking along the road. *On your way to the Pure Land then, Granny?*, the Zen master quipped condescendingly. The old lady nodded. *Amida Buddha will be waiting for you*, I suppose? The old lady shook her head vigorously. *What, Amida Buddha not in his Pure Land! Where is he then?* Gently the old lady tapped her heart twice, then continued on her way. *There's a real Pure Lander!* the Zen master said to himself.

In 1984, during the closing years of totalitarianism in the Soviet Union, Tengiz Abuladze, directed and produced the enigmatic Georgian film *Repentance* that portrayed the struggle and legacy of challenging tyrants like Stalin. It was a forbidden fruit until 1987 when censorship was lifted and crowds flocked to see it in Moscow. The film ends as it begins with a woman in a roadside kiosk making cakes in the shape of churches. An old woman asks her: *Is this the way to the church? This road is the road of a dictator*, the cake maker replies, *it does not lead to the church. What is the use of a way that does not lead to the church?* the old woman mutters as the film ends. Or in Buddhist terms: what is the use of a Way that does not lead to the Pure Land on the Other Shore? I believe that the way of materialism and consumption is a way of dictatorship that lends itself to suffering and is not a way to enlightenment.

As a Buddhist Quaker there are metaphysical questions about God and creation that like Buddha I have no inclination to answer. In response to such questions Buddha maintained silence in stillness. For him such questions were not as vital as our response to suffering through awakening to its causes that include ignorance, and through enlightenment to follow a path of liberation with noble compassion. I find that the sacred empowers that journey, a salvation of healing the wounds of experience, a salvation of peaceful supportive relationships. This is the ideal of a Quaker Meeting grounded on a common bedrock of faith, worship and service, and of a Buddhist Sangha, the company of those who seek to practise the way of Buddha.

What is it, I ask myself, that distinguishes Quaker worship from meditation or contemplation? In worship I sense the divine presence, the Sacred, thank and praise it, wait expectantly upon it, and attend to the promptings of love and truth in my heart. Buddhist practice of meditation and contemplation helps me still my body and mind, enables me to be fully present where I am. Through being in touch with my breathing in and breathing out, I give thanks for the gift of life and all that other beings have given me, and the unique gifts that I can bring to other sentient beings and to the care and nurture of the Earth and its resources.

The exercise of social engagement whether in a Buddhist or a Quaker way requires for myself both a prologue and an epilogue of inner stillness and reflection. I seek to approach a Quaker Meeting for Worship with an adequate preparation of heart, mind and spirit in the hour or so beforehand. Whilst Quaker worship may be regarded as the simplest form of Christian worship requiring no preparation, just get your body to the Meeting House, and indeed there is no problem in that, in another sense it is the most demanding of Christian worship as it requires the previous nurture of heart, mind and spirit.

There is a story of Buddha reaching the mouth of the Ganges and finding a fisherman mending his nets on the shore of the ocean.

*What do you like about the ocean?, he is asked. I love the ocean for these reasons, he replied. The shore slopes gently into it and so it is easy to get my boat into and out of it. The ocean is always in the same place: you always know where to find it. The ocean does not hold on to a corpse but gently carries it to the shore. All great rivers flow into it, leaving their own names behind. Even though great rivers pour into the ocean, the ocean retains its level. Its water is always salty and contains beautiful corals and precious stones. The ocean is a home to very many livings things from the smallest to the greatest.*

Buddha used the sayings of the fisherman as a parable about the spiritual journey into the ocean of faith and hope: easy to enter into, yet having increasing depths of living being. A Quaker Meeting for Worship is like this ocean loved by the fisherman whom Buddha met.

The Buddhist emphasis on right view and right thought I find beneficial in giving me an enhanced appreciation of the Bible amongst other sacred writings. What matters for me is how I perceive beneficially a passage from it, interpreted in the here and now for me personally. I do not have to neglect it as often happens nowadays as it gathers dust at Quaker Meeting Houses. In their books Thay and the Dalai Lama reveal their profound knowledge of the gospels and I too find them illuminating my spiritual journey. What is remarkable about the gospels is that they are remarkable. The sayings of Jesus and stories about him portrayed there are primarily the interpretations and perceptions of people profoundly influenced by the Christ within, and secondarily the very blurred memory of the man Jesus himself. Few of those sayings and stories are authentic accounts of Jesus himself as recent scholarship has shown, but what is miraculous is how the gospel writers and their sources wrote what they did. The gospels appear to have been written thirty to sixty years after Jesus' execution, and possibly the oral transmission over these decades was more accurate than the hundreds of years that elapsed between the death of Buddha and the first writings about him, and yet the oral transmission from monks to monks may have been more faithful than the transmission of the Jesus story as there was no need to show that Buddha fulfilled any prophecy.

I have worked a little in war torn regions of the Balkans and the Caucasus where I valued as I do today some basic insights and practices of Buddhism, especially the three Refuges and the Four Noble Truths including the Eightfold Way. The recognition of suffering is the beginning of the Way of Buddha, not only the involuntary experience of sickness, dying and death, but the avoidable suffering that we cause to others by hurting and alienating them, and by the hurt that they do to us. The poisons that we exercise in our personal relationships are those of anger, hate, ignorance and delusion, and the good news of the Way of Buddha is that this suffering can be overcome and transformed if we discern their cause and follow an Eightfold Way to enlightenment and liberation.

This Eightfold Way is for me a way of eight steps to find a true compass point direction and an inner balance. As normally recited,

the first step is Right View that I prefer to state as **Beneficial Perception**: do we feel, see, and hear what is really to be felt, seen and heard? What is in my mind and being when I perceive what is to be perceived?, I often ask myself.

from Beneficial Perception flows the next four steps of **Beneficial Thought, Speech and Action**. Expanding thought beyond mere thought in the head, I include as the second step beneficial feeling and meditation,

within the third step of Beneficial Speech, I include how we communicate non-violently with each other, and by the fourth step of Beneficial Action I mean any outward journey arising from an inner journey.

I am often challenged by the fifth step on the Way, that of **Beneficial Livelihood**. For many years I enjoyed the rather rarefied profession of a university physicist and wondered how I could change my livelihood to one more beneficial to others. Having specialised as an undergraduate in pure and applied nuclear physics, my conscience was exercised about the improper use of that knowledge to build nuclear bombs. I was alarmed by the proliferation of such terrible weapons during the Cold War and yet I had perceived the dangers of a totalitarian regime during a three-week visit to the Soviet Union in 1957. However, I warmed to the peoples of the Soviet Union that I met then. These impressions became reconciled in 1982 when I retired from university life to work for Quaker Peace and Service particularly in its relations with the peoples of the Soviet Union and Communist Europe.

The exercise of this livelihood required a continual practice of the sixth step of **Beneficial Effort**.

The last two steps of **Beneficial Mindfulness and Beneficial Concentration** I have found to be particularly beneficial to life and limb, and to stillness and focus within my mind. They even help me to keep crockery unbroken, to remain focussed on the performance of music and plays, and to remember where I have left my spectacles or hearing aids without which my perception is impaired!

Each step of the Way is a jewelled node of an Indra's net whose connecting threads interrelates each step to the other. This illustrates the Buddhist belief in true emptiness: nothing has a separate self, everything is interrelated: this is because that is. This net also illustrates the initiative of Thay in establishing in Vietnam the Tiep Hien Order of Interbeing: Tiep means both to be in touch with, and to continue; Hien means to realise in the here and now.

I find that the practice of mindfulness and concentration can be exercised in every moment of life. To live fully in the present moment is to fully appreciate the now, and to let loose a nostalgia for the past or an apprehension about the future.

The Buddhist practice of walking meditation is for me an awakening and liberating experience by following the breadth in every step, to breathe in the gift of life in a step that does not bruise Mother Earth and to breathe out with the unique gift that each of us can bring to a troubled world. I associate this with a *Marking* of the first Secretary General of the United Nations, Dag Hammershold: *for what has been, thanks; for what is to come, yes,* when breathing in I say to myself thanks; when breathing out, yes. A Buddhist monk leads us with a mindfulness bell during early morning walking meditation in the Amida retreat in France. When the monk invites it to sound, we pause in our steps to look around and take in where we are in the present moment, before the bell invites us to walk a little further.

I have such a Buddhist bell or bowl that was given to me by an American Quaker whilst I lived in Moscow. It is hand fashioned in the foothills of the Himalayas. I once took it to four meetings with teenage Croats and Serbs who had been alienated by the violence of the Balkan wars in Eastern Slavonia. They had not been able to meet each other for five years. In a sensitive part of the meetings each person when given the Buddhist bell was invited to speak about what they personally had experienced during the war: many painful experiences were shared. From time to time during the day's gathering I invited the bell to sound and asked everyone to be still and centre down to their true selves. A few days after I had returned from one of these exercises I received from a participant an Email that was simply addressed to the bell and said: *thank you for your gift of stillness.*

I have found the exercise of the four Noble Truths including the Eightfold Way beneficial to my Quaker faith and practice. For instance, in entering into a Quaker Meeting for Worship, I am helped by my Buddhist Way to be still, gathered and focussed. I find it easier than before to discipline my grasshopper mind that wants to ramble from one little thought to another. I find it helpful to practise some form of walking meditation on my way to the Quaker Meeting: my preparation of heart and mind is thereby quickened.

For me the Way of Buddha and the Way of Christ are akin. I feel drawn to both. Quaker faith and practice for me acknowledges them both like two Buddhists meeting on a path greeting each other with hands held as lotuses about to bloom, and with bodies slightly bowed, greetings practised in the East. As on signposts on the way to Tibet, *Om-mani-padme-hum, hail to the jewel in the heart of the lotus flower*, both Ways acknowledge the jewel of Love and Truth at the heart of all beings.

**Books referred to in this essay**, most of which have been subsequently reprinted:

Caroline Brazier (2003), Buddhist Psychology.
David Brazier (2001), The New Buddhism.
Thich Nath Hahn (1995), Living Buddha, Living Christ.
Thich Nath Hahn (1991), Old Path, White Clouds (a biography of the Buddha).
Thich Nath Hahn (1975), The Miracle of Mindfulness.

**The Author**

Peter Jarman was employed by Quaker Peace and Service as Europe Secretary from 1982 to 1991 when with his wife Roswitha he served as a Quaker representative in Russia. He and his wife have travelled widely amongst the peoples of Eastern Europe and the former Soviet Union, especially amongst the Muslim peoples of the North Caucasus. Before 1982 he was a teacher and research worker of physics and complementary studies in universities and research centres in Britain, Australia, the USA and Switzerland. He was Clerk of Quaker Action before retiring to the continual care community of Hartrigg Oaks in York. He is a Trustee of the Amida Trust that supports an international community of socially engaged Buddhists.

# Working with Quakers and Buddhists

## John A. McConnell

I WAS BROUGHT UP in the Church of Scotland. While I was interested in the something deeper that religion promised and was always ready to engage in discussion about it, I never felt at home with the beliefs and liturgy of that Church. In particular, the adolescent John resisted the concept of being led in prayer by a minister (since this seemed to interfere with the direct and personal nature of prayer) and argued inwardly with sermons from the pulpit. I do not mean this as a criticism, and of course my perception has changed – it is just how I saw it at the time.

One person I did feel I could relate to at that time was a young evangelical minister. I valued his emphasis on active commitment and his confidence in talking to God informally, as a normal father. I had problems with this too. Talking to God assumes some kind of mental understanding of Him. My kind minister happily filled this void with belief and devotion – but I just could not honestly do so.

Deep down I felt restless with certitudes that had to be believed before they could be experienced. I needed to begin to define life-quests rather than receive answers and the preoccupation with what should be believed seemed like a diversion into a cul-de-sac.

As a youth I liked to explore the rivers and woods near our home and would fish for hours along the banks of the Tweed. I had an uncle who was keen on field sports and he took me on shooting and fishing trips in Northern Ireland. Later, I acquired a small folding poacher's gun of my own and (sometimes legally, sometimes not) would shoot pigeon and rabbit. I felt somehow, at one with nature while I was stalking prey, and enjoyed the earthy tastes of trout, pigeon and rabbit.

However, there was a contradiction very obvious in retrospect, but not so clear at the time. On the one side I was genuinely kind to animals and wanted to be close to nature, while on the other I took enjoyment from hunting and killing them. This inner conflict would become evident only if my shots wounded a bird but did not kill it. That night I would lie awake trying to imagine the bird would be OK. Gradually, the shotgun came to be replaced by a camera.

Following these various pursuits – fishing, shooting, photography – I often found myself alone in the countryside. When I think back to mid-teenage years it was these times of stillness, when the 'hunt' was over or not begun, that I count as spiritual. Sitting by the banks of the River Tweed at sunset, and early-morning walks through the surrounding woodland, still evoke a sense of being special and of the mystery of life.

## Encounters with meditation and Meeting for Worship

I encountered first Buddhist meditation, and then Quaker meeting for worship within a few months of each other. I was in my early twenties and beginning post-graduate research in philosophy of religion. From the start, meditation and worship seemed variations on the single theme of stillness. Yes – they were interwoven with different concepts and beliefs, but they were both about using stillness as a way of spiritual exploration.

I began meditating using the Zen practice of just sitting. What attracted me about this was that one did not impose anything – no leading of thoughts or prayers – one just sat with awareness. It seemed diametrically opposite to all that I had resisted in Presbyterianism. For the first time in my life I had a way of spiritual exploration that I felt comfortable with – one I could work at. That is not to say I always felt comfortable with everything Buddhist – practising communities have their hierarchies and rituals too – but I found in meditation a rich spiritual resource. Since that time, around late 1972, I have meditated on a daily basis. Times and methods have varied, but meditation has become a part of life.

My introduction to Quakerism followed within six months or so. I remember my first meeting for worship very clearly. I had been attending a conference on philosophy of religion near Cambridge when a gentle elderly man by the name of Frederick Parker-Rhodes invited me to accompany him to Quaker meeting. When I said that I did not have the appropriate clothes, he replied, 'You come to a Quaker meeting just as you are.' It was the spirit that mattered, not the clothes.

The meeting began in silence and I remember thinking, from my brief experience of meditation, that the stillness had a good feel to it. The first ministry came from a man in his forties whose young daughter had (I think) leukaemia. He shared his agony as it was – honestly and powerfully. His vulnerability, and that of his family, pervaded the room. Silence followed, then more ministry. I do not remember what was said, but I do remember the absence of platitude, that each piece of ministry came from the heart, and the genuineness of the meeting. Then, something that seemed extraordinary at the time but I take for granted now as part of the dynamic of meeting – I found myself thinking things that blended perfectly with the words of others. I remember thinking it was as if the thoughts had flowed through us as a group.

There was a real sense of engagement of spirituality with the human condition and a level of sharing I had not experienced before. And this was worship! It could not have been further from the carefully tailored services that had so frustrated me in my teens. I became an attender at Lancaster Meeting the following Sunday, joined a small group of Quaker students who met in the university, and Quakerism has been an important part of my life and work ever since.

## An unexpected problem

Around late 1973, something happened, out of the blue – I began to experience problems with my vision. The first symptom was a blurred area in the visual field of the right eye. An old optician in Lancaster diagnosed it as a lazy eye and for some weeks I wore a patch over the left eye to make it work harder, and earned the nick-name, Piratical John. One day, I was walking in the university grounds when something as big and dark as a tree close-to filled my visual field. What I was seeing however was inside the eye, not outside. A clump of blood capillaries had torn from the retina and was swinging free in the jelly in the centre of the eye. Vision became soupy as the torn ends bled into the eye.

The condition, called Eale's Disease, is often associated with a brain tumour or diabetes, but I had neither. Best guesses at the time were that I had a genetic disposition to the condition or that there could be some underlying degenerative disease of which this was an early sign.

This brought a new fearfulness to life. I would wake up in the morning, look at the trees and sky outside my window, then notice the swirling mass of capillaries. Each day's symptoms seemed worse than the last. I put on a happy face but inwardly I was anxious. What would happen? What degenerative hell awaited? The future seemed dark.

While the cause remained unclear, it was possible to treat the symptoms. I took steroid eye-drops to prevent the capillaries over-producing and laser-shots to seal them when they bled. This appeared to stabilise the condition for a while, but it soon became apparent that it was not sustainable. Both steroids and laser-shots were doing long-term damage to the eye.

I told the consultant I wanted to discontinue the treatment. I remember his reply: 'You will probably bleed to blindness in about three years'. I guess the reader can imagine my despair. There seemed no way forward.

As it would happen I was in my first year of doctoral research on Existentialism and Mysticism, and could resonate with Existentialist concepts of the inherent meaninglessness of human existence. For the Existentialists, the meaning of life was not something there, waiting to be discovered – rather it was to be wrested from Being. How? By authentic choice, by facing the human condition without pretence. The Existentialist philosopher Martin Heidegger characterised human existence as 'thrown-ness' – we are and we have to be. We are beings whose meaning is in question. To live authentically is to take on that enigma – to question values rather than follow the herd, to accept insecurity rather than take refuge in pretence.

While it seemed likely that my condition would worsen as the consultant had predicted, at least I could *live* the situation authentically – that is, in as real and creative a way as possible, in a way that felt true. Reflecting on life as a whole, the stillness of meditation and meeting for worship was clearly the place to begin. I began to experiment with prayer and meditation. My condition became a kind of touchstone for spiritual depth of both. If meditation meant anything it had to tackle this suffering in a way that was not cosmetic, but real.

It was in this context that Buddha's teaching (the Dhamma) proved so valuable. Basically, it helped me engage systematically with suffering that was, till then, amorphous and unpredictable. Rather than being victim of the situation I began to actively engage. The Buddha himself was clear that this was the purpose saying, in response to academic philosophers, that his teaching is about suffering and liberation from suffering.

I would sit in meditation first thing in the morning and last thing at night. At the start, I found myself frequently distracted – sometimes by anxiety, sometimes by fantasy. Gradually I came to realise that the core of meditation is not the idealised enlightenment or calmness we might want to win, but a gentle inner wrestling with its own intrinsic depth.

It did not matter if meditations were not perfect. What did matter was that I engaged with all of my suffering.

What did I learn from the experiment? When I began meditating I thought something like this: 'If only I can get rid of the eye-problem, then I can be happy.' What I came to realise is that it is almost exactly the other way around: 'If I can be happy, then I can work with my eye-condition – and however it develops, it will not be such a problem.' I felt that whatever happened I could meet it with mindfulness.

Healing came, not as a miracle cure, but as something both less and more. It was something less in that symptoms have continued, though to a much lesser degree, to this day. It was something more in that the real change was the development of a sense of inner harmony which made the eye-disease seem out of place. I remember thinking that I had learned much from it. Now, I felt deeply that it just did not belong any more. The symptoms may get worse or better – I felt inwardly released from it.

The experiment gave me the confidence that spirituality was relevant to many areas of human suffering. Here was a practical resource touching attitudes and skills, but also deeper – relating to who we really are. The core of our existence is not the body, nor possessions, nor even mind. The core is that we *live* all of these. We can live reality in ways that enmesh us in conflict and suffering, or we can live the same set of circumstances in ways that lead to peace and happiness. We just need to experiment.

**Peace-making**

This gave a certain dynamism to the concept of looking for that of God in others. I remember my excitement at the discovery that Fox had used the word answer rather than look for (which was how I had originally heard it quoted):

*Then you will come to walk cheerfully over the world, answering that of God in everyone; whereby in them ye may be a blessing, and make the witness of God in them to bless you.*

This was, I felt, the foundation of peace-making – to use conflict as the opportunity to discover new depths in each other and ourselves.

I used meditation and worship in equal measure. While peace-making with Quaker Peace and Service in Sri Lanka, meeting for worship was a source of connection and strength. On the table were the Bible, Gita, Koran and the Dhammapada, and friends shared from their differing traditions – including a saintly Hindu who would quote from Tagore.

I would prepare for each difficult meeting with guerrillas, government ministers or whoever by practising mindfulness and extend loving-kindness to myself, to the people I was going to meet and to the long-suffering folk of Sri Lanka. The sensitivity and good-will that resulted often seemed to underpin our dialogue.

This sense that spirituality is a practical resource has also led to my current work with NGO's in Asia. My courses focus on peace-making, or healing, or dealing with anxiety. In the last twelve months participants have included Buddhist monks and nuns, cancer patients, doctors and nurses, Christian pastors, NGO activists, the staff of a prison which had experienced unrest, and policemen (Buddhist and Muslim) caught in a war situation. The kinds of suffering, and the related circumstances for these groups are of course widely different. What they have in common is that they all are lived and, as I said earlier, spirituality is about how we live them.

## The four noble truths

The teaching of the four noble truths, delivered in the first sermon after the Buddha's enlightenment, is basically a framework for spiritual engagement with suffering. This teaching was hugely important to me when I had my eye-problem. Today, I structure most of the courses I teach around it.

I explain it here in relation to healing, to peace-making – and reflect on parallels (or lack of them) in Quaker experience.

### The noble truth of suffering

The first noble truth is that suffering, *dukkha*, is a dimension of life. Several suttas record it:

> *Now this, monks, is the noble truth of suffering. Birth is suffering, ageing is suffering, death is suffering; sorrow, lamentation, pain, distress, and despair are suffering; association with the unbeloved is suffering, separation from the loved is suffering, not getting what is wanted is suffering. In short, the five clinging-aggregates (body, feeling, perception, mental compounding, consciousness) are suffering. In the Pali commentaries dukkha is explained as that which is hard to bear.*

Our natural tendency is to avoid really looking at suffering and we cope most of the time by solving problems externally. It is only when the usual remedies fail, and suffering threatens to undermine self in some way (that is, when it becomes hard to bear) that we begin to take its spiritual dimension seriously. My eye-problem was just such a crisis. External solutions in the shape of medical treatments had evaporated and I had times of deep despair about what the future might hold.

Similarly, it is when things get difficult in a conflict – perhaps when our strategies have proved ineffective, or when the conflict seems to be destroying what was valuable in a relationship, or when we feel bad about our own words and actions – that our focus shifts from things we can fix, to the nature of this suffering. I guess this happens around the point where we begin to ask, rhetorically: 'Is this really happening? Is it really me? What have I got myself into? Where is this going to end?' These are the kinds of questions associated with the first truth – but they are not rhetorical.

The Buddha said of the first truth that it '...is to be comprehended'. We need to get to know our suffering. Only then can we begin to deal with it. You might think, 'Of course I know my suffering! I experience it don't I?' Actually, we seldom do. Most of us have spent so much energy trying to avoid unpleasant feelings that avoidance is built into our perception. Then, when we do decide to confront suffering we will sub-consciously choose some identifiable problem, one we feel we can face, and ignore a broader sense of disorientation and futility that we feel we can't.

Quakers are generally quite good at being open to suffering. The early Quaker emphasis on the importance of one's condition in discerning truth is still with us today, and I remember many sharings of vulnerabilities in meetings for worship. When a small group of us set up a meeting for healing there were intimate sharings of suffering related to ill-health – and deeply healing periods of worship after.

If we listen, rather than speak, our prayer also gives space for suffering to come to awareness and stay as long as is needful. There is no liturgy to move it on so to speak. Allowing unease and uncertainty to develop in this way is part of Quaker discernment.

The exception seems, strangely, to be conflict. Quakers seem quite good at developing a level of sensitivity and considerateness that keeps us from hurting each other and getting into conflict in the first place. There are many occasions too, when a Friend will call for a time of quiet amid a heated meeting – with positive results. However, once in conflict, Quakers are not so good at engaging with the suffering.

In my twenty-odd years as a Friend I have observed a number of conflicts in different settings – some in Quaker meetings, some in Quaker organisations. Most get resolved constructively at an early stage, but some do not – and some of the strategies used are clearly oriented to avoidance of suffering. Quakers have chosen to be quietly stubborn, holding our position in a superior way; move on from rather than deal with upsetting issues; worship separately from our conflictants, thus avoiding the awkwardness of dealing with the problem at a spiritual level; maintain a superficial politeness while harbouring feelings of hurt and blame, thus avoiding sensitive issues and the feelings they would trigger; explain the conflict by the difficult personalities of our conflictants or by their failure really to understand/practise Quaker process, thus avoiding awareness of our own self-centred view of the situation.

The result of all these strategies is to avoid engagement with the conflict – that is to avoid taking it on as a spiritual challenge.

### Meditation and the first noble truth

The Buddhist way of knowing suffering is to be mindful of the present moment. We don't try to evoke suffering – just observe what is. In fact, when we meditate, this is exactly what happens. We put light concentration on breathing and then just try to be mindful of whatever arises. After a period when things may seem to go well the old suffering begins to intrude – and so do our old habits of avoidance. Following the first noble truth we try to know the suffering more deeply. So we just observe the feeling without judgement, without trying to make ourselves feel better.

After a few sessions we begin to discern different dimensions of the experience.

### The simile of the two arrows

The Buddha identifies what he means by suffering, and what Dhamma could achieve, in the simile of the two arrows. He poses a question: since those who practise Dhamma, and those who do not, both experience the same range of feelings (pleasant, unpleasant and neutral) what is the difference between them? He identifies two kinds of suffering – discomfort and anxiety:

> *Bikkhus, when the person who does not know Dhamma is being contacted by a painful feeling, he sorrows, grieves, and laments; he weeps, beating his breast and becomes distraught. He feels two feelings – a bodily and a mental one. Suppose they were to strike a man with an arrow, and then they would strike him immediately afterwards with a second arrow, so that the man would feel a feeling caused by two arrows. So too, when the person who does not know Dhamma is being contacted by a painful feeling ... he feels two feelings – a bodily one and a mental one.*

The first arrow represents physical discomfort and we can extend it to mean that element of suffering that just happens. For me, the daily silhouettes of the tangle of capillaries, the soupy vision and the resultant eye-strain was one such dimension – physical suffering. For those in conflict the first arrow could include hearing an insult, loss of something precious to us, and so on. These all happen to us. We may or may not have contributed to the event, but the event itself is not of our choosing.

The second arrow has to do with our mental reaction to the first. I began to notice an array of mental suffering about the disease. This ranged from frustration (at not being able to read without straining the good eye), through various anxieties (about whether symptoms were getting better or worse), to a sense of hopelessness about the future.

For someone in conflict, anxiety about losing face, agony about deterioration of a close relationship, frustration and fury at what the other side seems to be able to get away with are all instances of mental suffering.

One species of mental suffering for Quakers is revulsion at the fact that conflict is taking place within the Quaker community. There is a feeling that this simply ought not to be happening. When it continues there is a despair that the conflict is undermining the quality of our spirituality as a meeting.

From a Buddhist point of view, it is this second arrow that we can, most effectively, begin with.

There are parallels between mindfulness and the prayer of stillness in Christian experience. Jesus taught that we should make our suffering into prayer, not obscure it with pretence and pride.

We can see something of this in the parable of the tax-gatherer and the Pharisee. The highly respected Pharisee prays in the centre of the temple while the tax gatherer, despised as collaborator and fraudster, sobs in the corner. The Pharisee prays: *God, I thank Thee that I am not like other men, extortioners, unjust, adulterers, or even like this tax collector. I fast twice a week, I give tithes of all that I get.* The tax-gatherer's prayer is different: But the tax collector, standing far off, would not even lift up his eyes to heaven, but beat his breast, saying, *God, be merciful to me a sinner!* The Pharisee exalts in his own goodness and his prayer reflects his self-satisfaction. The tax-collector on the other hand has the simplest of prayers and allows his experience to speak the rest. It was the tax-collector, who had sinned much but was in touch with his suffering, who went home with his suffering resolved – not the more respectable Pharisee.

### The noble truth of the origin of suffering

When we try to meditate we discover that, far from the quiet refuge we might have imagined, it is difficult. The mind wanders and we find ourselves caught up in countless habits – daydreaming, weaving stories around feelings, clinging to this, resisting that. The second noble truth is that a major cause of suffering lies in just these mental habits:

> *And this, monks, is the noble truth of the origination of suffering: the craving that makes for further becoming – accompanied by passion and delight, relishing now here and now there – i.e. craving for sensual pleasure, craving for becoming, craving for non-becoming.*

The fact that such habits arise in meditation is important. Ordinarily our minds focus on objects – something we want, the event we remember, the face of someone who has insulted us – and we simply do not see the related mental process. Following the second noble truth we broaden our focus, and so begin to take note of mental processes too – the quality of wanting and feelings that precipitate it, the way we select the event to remember and the feelings it arouses, the way we mentally put together information to form a picture of our conflictant and so on. Behind every external object lies a complex subjective mechanism.

These habits do not come up at a comfortable distance, nor even close-by – they appear from within. The memory of the person who insulted us arises and we feel angry, right there, while we are meditating. Automatically, we get caught up in the old cycle of resentment and blame.

The tendency is quickly to suppress the distraction and bring attention back to breathing, perhaps to blame ourselves for being angry or for not meditating properly. However, the moment we realise we are caught up, we are already mindful. So, following the second truth, we can be mindful of the current fragment of thinking and feeling, and just be still within it. Gently we bring attention to breathing, but are careful not to exclude anything. We want to overcome suffering through depth of awareness – not ignorance.

Back in the 1970s, I began to discern some of the mental habits that were feeding my misery. There were several dimensions to this, one of which was how I was reacting to symptoms each day. The misery-go-round went something like this: first thing in the morning I would automatically look for the silhouette of the tangle of capillaries, then feel afraid. I would wonder if it was worse than yesterday, squint again, decide it was probably larger, and feel more fear. On the basis of this fear I would begin to imagine what lay ahead, what blindness would be like, and how it would interfere with having either career or family. Gradually, I would begin to feel tired and hopeless. Then, there was the lurking issue of a degenerative disease. This had come in an off-hand remark by the consultant, but I worried until it became near certain reality.

Much of the Buddha's psychology is intended to help identify unskilled mental habits just like these. Sometimes he does this in terms of tendencies, sometimes in terms of sequences of mind-body states.

### Sequences of states

Without going into too much detail, we can see such a sequence in the above anxiety process:
- The mind's contact with an object (the symptom)
- Feeling (upset)
- Craving (thirst to change things)
- Mental grasping (as the mind clings to a particular outcome)
- Projection of self and reality (as the thoughts that have preoccupied us imperceptibly become seen as reality)
- Then suffering (as we live life from this dysfunctional self-identity).

I remember my amazement at realising that my own pattern of thinking, much of it semi-conscious, was actually a cause of my suffering. Yes—the eye-disease was a problem, but it was *not* the main cause. The anxiety-process itself was the immediate cause – and that had a totally different logic.

In the same way, with mindfulness we can begin to notice patterns in the way thought, feeling and behaviour follow each other, both within our own mind-body and in our relations with others. This opens up a new dimension in conflict where unthought reactions to feeling often shape our behaviour. As these patterns are brought to awareness, we gain the chance to change our approach.

### Tendencies

The Buddha also analysed mechanisms leading to suffering in terms of tendencies. One such list, widely known in

Buddhist countries, is the *akusala-mula* (the unhealthy roots of action) – *lobha* (restless greed), *dosa* (hate or resentment), and *moha* (deluded understanding).

You can take any conflict and see lobha, dosa and moha interacting, both within and between conflictants, right through it. To make peace is primarily to undermine and transform these unhealthy roots.

It is important to stress that the *akusala-mula* are in no way terms of blame or judgement – they are there simply to help identify and deal with unskilful thinking.

*Moha (delusion – unmindful understanding)*

*Moha* is self-centred, often simplistic understanding. It contributes to fear in that, picturing self in a certain way, we then become afraid for the picture. For example, because we have been healthy until now we assume that we will continue to be healthy – as if good health is somehow part of who we are. This makes us vulnerable to events which suggest we are not healthy.

If we are diagnosed with a serious illness, for example, we do not believe the diagnosis initially. It simply contradicts the picture we have of ourselves – so our first reaction is to disbelieve it. I, for example, could not believe the evidence of my senses – that I had a serious eye-problem.

Later, if the diagnosis is confirmed, our minds add another picture: now that we are ill we are sure to get much worse. We see self now as something like a doomed-victim and start looking for symptoms of decline. Both of these are deluded pictures of reality.

With two such contrary pictures of reality, we flit from one to the other, sometimes hopeful, more often fearful – and become increasingly anxious.

Delusion in conflict lies in that we think we understand both ourselves and the other – and that we are in the right. With some selective observation we can portray self as good, and the other as basically selfish and unreasonable. Even when we make mistakes we can blame them on the enemy for they made us react like that.

There is a particularly Quaker version of delusion which runs something like this: We are peace-loving people. Indeed, we make peace all over the world. We just cannot be in conflict ourselves. Here, peace becomes a prized quality of self, something we possess – an adjunct of the ego.

Another element of Quaker *moha*, resulting in part from our success in contributing to peace in the world, is that we tend to think of peace in terms of external relations between people – the ceasing of all wars and fighting – rather than inner peace of mind and spirit.

These two combine to create the sad paradox that, while we are very enthusiastic about peace-making in the world, we frequently do not take conflict within our community as a spiritual challenge – and so miss the opportunity to learn from it. By affirming self as Quaker and therefore peaceful we lose the peace that opens when we use the turmoil to let go defence of self and trust to the spiritual depth we know in worship. This was the problem of the Pharisee, and it is often ours too.

*Lobha (greed – unmindful wanting)*

All of us have some degree of attachment to possessions, privileges, lifestyles, activities, and so on – attachments that are reinforced by habitual unmindful wanting taking place each day. When any of these are threatened we experience a degree of fear and insecurity as if the threat was against our person.

The kind of *lobha* that arises is influenced by our self-picture. As a result of the earlier *moha* that we are healthy, we become greedy for indications that the diagnosis is wrong, or that the illness is receding. Then, presuming the new self-picture of doomed-victim we EXPECT that the condition will worsen and feel we have to hunt for indications that it is getting worse (one kind of *lobha*), yet desire reassurance that it will not (another kind of *lobha*).

*Lobha* in conflict often operates at various levels. There is the matter at issue, whether the fence is here or three feet to the side, and then there is perhaps greed to be dominant, and fear of losing status if the other side wins.

A common Quaker *lobha* in conflict is to get it behind us, to forgive and forget, move on – so that we can rebuild interpersonal relationships again. This is not bad of course – just it tends to leave unresolved issues in its wake. Clinging to this aim we tend to ignore disturbing issues and feelings that the conflict has touched. The same patterns then recur when the next conflict presents itself.

## *Dosa (hate – unmindful attitude)*

*Dosa* is a self-centred, resentful attitude to life where we are ready to blame self and others when things are not to our satisfaction. We may blame ourselves for somehow causing the illness, the doctors for not being able to cure it, or carers for not looking after us properly.

Again *moha* is a powerful influence. If we picture self as perfect and the illness as alien then we will resent it, resent our situation and feel alienated from our body.

In conflict the *moha* of being in the right affects our attitude to the other side. If we are right then they are the cause of the problem. Our attitude becomes resentful and this is expressed in our behaviour.

For Quakers, the belief that we possess the quality of peacefulness, that we should be peaceful, makes it difficult to accept feelings of hurt and anger, and inhibits us from expressing them effectively. We tend to project them onto the difficult or unQuakerly character of our conflictant. This can lead to enduring stand-offs with each side quietly but implacably convinced they are right and the other wrong.

## *The use of psychological analyses*

These concepts are not intended to categorise others, but to work more effectively at our own self-liberation. Whichever means of analysis is used, the aim is the same. The Buddha described the purpose of the second noble truth as follows: 'This noble truth of the origination of suffering is to be abandoned'. That is, when an unhealthy mental habit is there in our experience we have the chance to let it go. That we are caught up in the distraction is an opportunity. We cannot let go of attachment in the abstract. We need it there in experience, tugging at our minds, in order to let go. Meditation is a constant process of noticing clinging and letting go. The purpose of psychological analysis is to facilitate this process.

Talking of his own experience, the Buddha said that before his enlightenment he experienced ill-will. Then, becoming mindful of it, he could see that it was causing annoyance to himself and to others, that it led away from *nibbana* (cessation of craving). Realising this, he could lay ill-will down.

Analysis into sequences of states is valuable too. Let's say we experience anxiety. If we are mindful we will soon find that there is a process powered by feelings of fear. When we try to be mindful of this fear we find ourselves distracted by images of what might happen, and these create ever more stress. So, we have observed a sequence: fear, images of the future, more fear. Knowing this we can be especially mindful when fear next arises.

When it does we are mindful, perhaps concentrating lightly on breathing, perhaps praying through it. We feel the tendency to imagine futures – but we just let it be, let it go. The sure effect will be that this time the fear will not go over into imagination and stress. The fear is there, but we are still in the midst of it.

We learn to trust our sense of deepening awareness. Rather than suppress fear, awareness releases from it – transcends it. We are meeting reality in a new way – from deep awareness rather than from self. There is a sense of the reality of Spirit, not as object of perception or devotion and certainly nothing we can possess. There is just the sense that, when all that is conditioned falls away, this is who we ultimately are.

There is something real and powerful about this, something relevant to the whole of life. It empowers us to heal in the midst of sickness, to make peace in face of hostility. I remember sitting with the Quaker poet Dorothy Nimmo shortly before she died. While physically very weak, and well aware that she was dying, she had a lovely – I have to say radiant – smile: 'I could be very, very afraid, but that's not a road (I want to go down). I've discovered, what it's all about is learning to rest in God's infinite love.' The fear was there, but it was a stepping-stone to release, and a new closeness to God. By letting go of the compulsion to resist, we let go of self, and discover a depth of awareness, a reality of spirit, we could not possibly imagine.

And that, essentially, is the second noble truth. Yes – it is part of Buddhist psychology, but it is also universal

We all make mistakes, we all get entangled in foolishness, and we all have a lot we need to release. Times of prayer and meditation that are calm and happy are fine – but so are those where we encounter difficulty. In responding to his son, Rahula, who had been having difficult experiences in meditation, the Buddha advises him to let his meditation be like water, like earth, like fire and like the wind:

> *Rahula, develop meditation that is like water ... Just as people wash clean things and dirty things, excrement, urine, spittle, pus and blood in water but the water is not horrified, humiliated, disgusted because of that, so too, Rahula, develop meditation that is like water; for when you develop meditation that is like water, arisen agreeable and disagreeable contacts will not invade your mind and remain.*

Like water, meditation penetrates, washes and refines the on-going stream of consciousness. Gently it flows into difficult areas, first exposing, then washing away those processes that are destructive. This process of refinement happens at different levels and it is not unusual to find issues, long submerged, suddenly appear during meditation. This can be painful, but deeply healing.

I mentioned that I used to shoot and fish as a youth, pastimes that continued into my student years – and until the following event occurred.

Once, about a year after I had begun practising, I was meditating when I found myself caught up in a very vivid spontaneous visualisation – like a strong day-dream. In the visualisation, I was looking along the barrels of my shot-gun, following a rabbit as it ran across a field. Next moment, the barrels were facing me. I was scared! My hair stood on end. It wasn't that I mistook the image for reality, but the visualisation related directly to my condition. You see, it was my finger that was on trigger. The reason for the fear was that I did not trust myself. I felt devastated. I sat, battered and aware as memories and feelings came tumbling through. I think I have never been so humbled.

The visualisation had happened in a few moments but the effect was to lift a burden permanently from my back – one that I did not even know I carried. I sold one gun, took the firing pins out of the other, and never fired at a living thing again. Later in life I took my sons fishing when they asked, but with the condition that we throw back everything we caught.

Two years ago we started to keep poultry, and I was very pleased to overhear my daughter saying to the newly arrived, and slightly edgy, hens: 'there's no need to worry, we're all vegetarians!'

### *The noble truth of the cessation of suffering*

The third truth is that cessation of attachment results in reduction of suffering. However hopeless things seem, if we can undermine the mental habits that feed our despair, then the suffering will reduce. This happens naturally. Freed from the demands and distortions of self-centredness, deep awareness is naturally wise and deeply caring. Its natural tendency is to bring into harmony – it is tremendously healing.

And what to do with this third truth? The Buddha says it is to be realised, attained in our daily lives. I don't see this as all or nothing. You can experience it for yourself – let go a habit of clinging, rest in awareness, and you can feel the difference. It is not final liberation of course, but it is quite real.

The out-working of this third truth is that we begin to see our suffering in a different way. Yes, there is the disease, but we know it as dis-ease in the context of a much deeper harmony, and can work at bringing things back into balance. Yes, there is conflict, but we know it as a tangle of unskilful thought and action in the context of an altogether broader inner peace – and so we can work with it to make peace.

Deeper awareness discloses fresh possibilities. In place of greed we become attuned to the real needs of ourselves and the world, in place of hate we experience compassion and can experiment with loving-kindness, in place of self-centred delusion we begin to understand life more deeply, more clearly.

Though Quakers use different words, we experience these same dimensions of transformation in meeting for worship. Sitting with unease in silent worship brings us to a place where habitual avoidances and pretences fall away, and stillness deepens. Understanding becomes more open, we often see things in different ways, and leadings arise in the stillness. We often experience a freshness about life as a result – an enthusiasm to engage, to experiment. This shift in attitude, understanding and faith then affects how we work with, and feel about, the world.

In terms of the parable of the two arrows, the person who is aware is hit by the first (the discomfort or misfortune) just the same, but avoids the second (does not make it into a fraught despairing self-centred drama).

## *The fourth noble truth: the Eightfold Way of Enlightenment*

A key element in any spiritual endeavour is daily practice. The fourth noble truth outlines eight aspects of daily practice that will help lead to the cessation of self-centred mental habits, and so to a reduction of suffering itself. They are not rules to be obeyed so much as guidelines to be considered as we reflect on our practice. They are not unlike Advices and Queries. Policemen will decide differently from nurses: we apply it to our individual situations.

What is the eight-fold path for Quakers in conflict? I incorporate some of my own reflections:

### *Right understanding:*

Suffering and conflict are both normal and relate directly to self-centred habits of mind. For sure, our own unskilful mental habits contribute to it. We can assume that. So we should understand the fact that we are in conflict as an opportunity to experiment spiritually.

With mindfulness in worship and daily life we become more sensitive to these semi-conscious processes in ourselves and others. While these self-centred habits are there in our hearts and minds, we have the opportunity to meet them with awareness rather than defence. The comments of others (especially our conflictants) probably hold some truth and should be welcomed rather than rejected. We try to attend to the plank in our own eye rather than the splinter in the other's.

As we come to understand ourselves better, so we become able to trust to a sense of inner peace, and relate more sensitively to others. We find we feel better about things too – willing to explore differences rather than defend self.

We can live life in such a way that we make human interaction an experiment in acceptance, awareness and love.

### *Right thought:*

Healthy thought is a very important resource in being healer and peace-maker. Cultivation of selfless energy (like loving-kindness and compassion) help us replace the alienation that results from fear. We learn to live wisely and harmoniously – and thus bring happiness to others.

***Right speech:***
Right speech is, first and foremost, to listen. When we speak we should be mindful and have in mind the benefit of the other. Anxiety and isolation work the same way in them as they do in us ... so with mindful words we can help each other find peace.

***Right action:***
We can experiment in dealing with our problems – draw on our insight and compassion. Where there is fear we need to take action so that we confront the fear rather than run from it. We can show our kindness and commitment in our actions more effectively than say it sometimes.

***Right livelihood:***
We can review the pattern of our lives. Are there areas we feel uneasy about? Are they related to our fear and anxiety? Maybe we can change them.

***Right effort:***
It takes effort to change the way we live life, especially since mental habits are often largely unconscious. Then, every time anxiety comes up during the day, we need to become mindful of it. Anxiety, intolerance, isolation all grow in small cycles, one built upon the other – and that is exactly how we have to deal with them. We need to make the effort to be mindful of each experience – let it be, let it go. Gradually, we learn to respond from awareness rather than from self.

***Right mindfulness:***
Mindfulness is the key to spiritual freedom. We need ways of meditation and prayer that are open to our suffering, open to our faults. Then, as we discern habits of attachment we have the chance to release them in faith – without clinging or resisting let them be there in experience, and let them go.

### *Right concentration:*

Concentration is like the Quaker technique of centring down. It should be sufficient to keep the mind still, but not so much as to exclude distractions. Rather the key function of concentration is to become mindful in the midst of the distraction. Stillness in the midst of the tendency to react is the stepping-stone to inner peace.

## Mutual learnings

Because my focus is helping the people who come on my courses I tend to think in terms of resources they can use. So here are some strengths from both traditions which it would be good to see more of in the world.

One important resource in Quakerism is the way words shared in the silence get translated into experimental living by the individual or the group. Just such an active interface between spirit and daily life is something we could all learn from.

As I said earlier, modern Quakers are so focussed on peace in the world that we sometimes lack a sense of inner peace. We need to take the inner turbulence of conflict as a spiritual challenge, and let it deepen rather than disrupt our worship.

Then, in a Buddhist analysis, the sparky interactions that create the bad feeling, and which we nurse grievances about, derive from much longer-indulged patterns of thinking and behaviour. It is when the negative thought is actually there that we need to know it and let go – and the only way I know to do that is with a daily practice.

Individual Quakers may well have such practices, but it seems not to be something that we share and discuss with each other. One resource from Buddhism therefore, is the tradition of personal meditation practice and retreats. Then, Buddhists talk with *kalayanamitra* (spiritual friends) about spiritual experiences in meditation and daily life. There is an element of this in ministry during meeting, and in discussion groups oriented to spirituality – just that we could give it more emphasis.

Back to the paradox of the peacemakers who have such difficulty with our own conflict, one reason might be that we don't have the language to analyse the internal dimension of conflict. We are familiar with concepts and skills of conflict resolution, but when they don't move things on we still have to deal with our inner turmoil. If we can't work with this spiritually, we will find it difficult to relate to our conflictant without slipping into habits of aloofness and inhibition. One resource from the Buddha's teaching, which would be very useful to us, is its marvellous spiritual psychology. This can help us analyse unhealthy mind-states – our own, not others – and get our contribution to the situation as sensitive and compassionate as possible. The language is neutral and the intention is solely to liberate, not to judge.

## Conclusion

I have practised, studied, and worked closely with Buddhists and Quakers for more than thirty years. I know many of our faults, but I also know the deep and lovely spirituality that I find, regularly and in abundance, in both communities.

Participants on my courses sometimes cannot work out if I am one or the other. In truth I have to say I am both. Meditation is part of my life, Meeting is part of my life. I have benefited hugely from the teachings of Buddha and of Jesus – and the sensitivity and sharing of both faith communities.

There are various comparisons and contrasts to be made but the greatest commonality between the two faiths has to do with the universal spirituality to which they both point. May we become still, open to awareness here and now, and experiment with it in our own lives.

## The Author

John McConnell has been involved with the Religious Society of Friends since the early 1970s. His doctoral research was on mysticism and existentialism. Following some years teaching religious studies, he worked for Quakers as peace education adviser in the early 1980s, then with his wife Erica as regional representative for Quaker Peace and Service in Sri Lanka. Since then he has worked mostly with Buddhist NGOs in Asia, exploring ways in which spirituality (particularly using Buddhist psychology) can be applied to difficult areas of life. He is currently writing a book on Buddhist psychology and healing.

# Flirting with the Buddha

## Jonathan Fryer

ENLIGHTENMENT OR awareness is an attractive concept. I suspect most of us have been striving for it at one stage or another in our lives. Awareness of ourselves, certainly, but even more awareness of the human condition, in relation to the universe and eternity. It is not surprising that this should be so amongst Quakers, as so many of us would define ourselves as seekers: seekers after Truth, insofar as anything so abstract can exist. In this way, life is a spiritual journey, along which one meets many ideas and many people, each offering an example to be pondered in tranquillity. Sometimes these ideas and individuals influence us, sometimes not. And in my own case, for a long time, it was Buddhism that has offered the most food for thought.

I am a child of the Vietnam generation. As radicalised adolescents in the late 1960s, we marched and sat in on campuses and in the streets, in Britain and elsewhere, as the War hung above our heads like some great black cloud. Day after day, not for months but for years, the terrible black-and-white images of conflict and human suffering flickered on our TV screens, or glared from our newspapers. Unlike Tony Blair over Iraq, Harold Wilson kept Britain out of the Vietnam theatre, yet some of the anger of the students and others who protested against the War was directed at British politicians, for passively endorsing the US-led neo-imperialist venture. And because the Americans appeared to be wrong, many young Britons assumed that the Communist North

Vietnamese and their Viet Cong partners in the South must be right.

I couldn't see things in such black-and-white terms. I couldn't hold posters of North Vietnam's leader aloft, chanting enthusiastically 'Ho! Ho! Ho Chi Minh!' There were aspects of Communism, and the totalitarian nature of Communist regimes, that offended my liberal sensibilities. But what could I know from the sheltered fastness of my sixth-form block at school in Manchester? Though I scoured every relevant piece that appeared in the media, I decided the only way to make up my own mind about the War was to go out there and see things for myself. Even before I left, I half suspected that this would be a search for answers to questions much broader than the issues of this particular War, about peace and development and cultural relativism, as well as about my own sense of identity and purpose. Surprisingly, the headmaster had no objections to my departing before the end of the school year. In fact, he seemed quite relieved to get rid of me. Armed with letters of accreditation from *The Manchester Evening News* and *The Geographical Magazine*, both of which had been remarkably positive when approached by a schoolboy hoping overnight to become a reporter, I set off overland.

Thus it was, a couple of months later, that I found myself standing in the arrivals hall of Saigon's Ton Sa Nhut airport, a small YMCA bag slung over my shoulder, wondering what on earth I would do next. Just getting there had been the focus of my energy, and I had given little consideration to the practicalities of actually being there. The YMCA bag was a legacy of an earlier commitment to the Anglican Church and associated bodies. I had gone through a short period of intense religious devotion at around the age of puberty, getting confirmed and regularly attending 8 o'clock Communion at the local parish church. But soon disillusionment had set in, as the Church of England increasingly struck me as preposterous, as I studied more of its history (including the reasons for its founding) and listened to what many of its clergy, including our local vicar, were saying. However, the YMCA had good facilities which I continued to patronise long after I had suspended my faith, and the bag I had brought with me to Saigon would now change the course of my life.

As the swirl of US and Vietnamese military and civilians diminished around me at the airport, a very English voice penetrated my daze, asking me if I was alright. The youngish man in black shirt and trousers who had spoken was looking at me quizzically. He introduced himself as a quintessentially Anglican being: the Rural Dean of South East Asia. He had been seeing his pregnant wife off on a plane to Singapore, where she would give birth, away from the stress of the War. Gesturing towards my YMCA bag, he said that if I did not have a place to stay, I was welcome to go home with him and use his spare bedroom until I found my feet. At 19, and on the road, one easily, indeed eagerly, accepts the hospitality of strangers.

The following day was a Sunday. At breakfast my host tentatively asked whether I would like to accompany him to his church. When I declined, he generously suggested a couple of alternatives. If I turned left out of his villa, he explained, I would find a small Ba'hai centre, while if I turned right, there was a Quaker Meeting that took place in the living room of a British doctor who worked in one of the local hospitals. I had no experience or knowledge of either of these two groups, but turned right, and soon found myself sitting in silence amongst a dozen or so people of different nationalities. Only a few minutes into the Meeting for Worship, there was an almighty crash from a shell that fell not far away. Nobody flinched.

Among the attenders at that first Meeting for Worship were a couple of people who worked with Buddhist groups in Saigon. Some of the more radical Buddhist monks were then taking a stand against the War and were involved in community activities that aroused the ire of the deeply corrupt and authoritarian South Vietnamese government. Such political activism surprised me, as I had always envisaged Buddhist monks as being detached from the world, sitting in the lotus position, straining to reach Nirvana. Yet here in Saigon were some young men in saffron robes intervening in the political process. In the most extreme cases, some would indeed sit in the lotus position, in the middle of the street, then pour petrol over themselves and set themselves alight, burning to death as passers-by stared in shock and awe. This was not just a good journalistic story. It was deeply unsettling. And it prompted me to begin to study the Buddha's teaching, as well as the example of his own life, to see if I could learn anything about my own condition.

Indeed, when I returned to England and went up to university, I quickly abandoned the geography course for which I had been accepted, and switched to Chinese and Japanese studies instead, largely so I could study some Buddhist texts in the original. I suppose with the naivety of youth I thought that if I understood the language, I would understand the meaning, whereas the more I studied, the more impenetrable it all appeared. There were some laymen's guides to the subject, such as Christmas Humphrey's Pelican Original *Buddhism*, that at least gave one some comprehensible context. But painstakingly reading sutras in Chinese, character by obscure character, did my head in. Sometimes I was tempted to give up, but then reflected that I could hardly expect to persuade the college authorities to let me change subject again. Knowing that Buddhist monks in Asia spent their whole lives – often from infancy – trying to achieve enlightenment was in itself deeply discouraging. How could I hope to get anywhere, juggling my studies with the everyday challenges of life in a university, not to mention the various experiments in human relationships in which I had, in typical undergraduate fashion, become involved?

I found a glimmer of hope in Zen. This Japanese refinement of an earlier Chinese school of Buddhism was doubly appealing. First, it had inspired artistic expression – ranging from calligraphy to gardens – of powerful simplicity that chimed with my own developing aesthetic. And second, it offered the prospect of instant enlightenment through a sudden flash of realisation, which might come at any moment. Zen masters tried to induce this amongst their pupils, by shock tactics such as a sudden clip round the ear, or by exhorting them to hear the sound of one hand clapping. Anyone might be lucky enough to have this experience. But one needed to be properly prepared.

The Buddha himself, about 2,500 years ago, had reportedly had such a flash of awareness one night while sitting under a tree (delightfully named *ficus religious*). But this was only after many years of wandering and false starts. The son of an affluent family, in the lowlands of what is now Nepal, he had become the original Dharma Bum, travelling the roads of northern India, begging for food when necessary, alternately meditating and exchanging ideas with other religiously inclined beings. For a while the Buddha had tried the route of self-mortification, fasting so severely that his ribs stuck out, before realising that this was not the true path, but instead a form of self-indulgence. Learning about that was a huge relief to me. Though I had become a vegetarian in South East Asia, in the belief that other sentient beings were sacred, I did not fancy starving myself into some higher state of consciousness. Deep into the night, in my lodgings in North Oxford, I read on about the Buddha's life, fuelling my body with mint sauce sandwiches.

There was, however, one uncomfortable, inescapable fact that was emerging from my studies, and that was that renunciation was central to the whole Buddhist discourse. In order to gain awareness, one needed to give up almost everything else. Buddha had renounced the material benefits and social status of his background, and Buddhist monks renounced most of what one might consider normal life, including family and friends, embracing poverty and an existence based in mendicancy.

The concept of a mendicant's life particularly bothered me. I had seen monks going round with their begging bowls, particularly in Thailand. And although the faithful eagerly filled them with food – doubtless convinced that they would achieve merit by doing so – a word kept nagging my brain like a mosquito while I viewed the practice; and that word was 'parasite'. The monks' existence, at least in the towns, was only possible because other people provided for them. Moreover, many of the people doing so were genuinely poor, due to their circumstances, not out of a philosophical volition, and seemingly more in need of assistance than in a position to give handouts.

Such notions especially troubled me as I extended my field of studies into the history and culture of Tibet. I was appalled at what the Chinese were then doing in Tibet. As the Cultural Revolution raged, monasteries were being destroyed, and monks were forced to find other occupations and to marry. But I also understood the logic of the Chinese criticism of the traditional feudal society in Tibet, in which religious leaders held sway over an impoverished nation of serfs. I could not reconcile what I was reading about Tibet with the nobler aspects of the religious theory. By now, I was accustomed to the idea of Buddhism as a way of liberating people from suffering, but if what some of the Chinese commentators – and Western travellers – were saying was true, then some of the suffering was actually imposed by Tibet's theocracy.

Always a believer in hearing things from the horse's mouth, I decided that I would ask the Dalai Lama. The Society of Friends – with whom I had established new contact when I returned to England from South East Asia – had received an invitation to send a representative to a tea party being organised for Tibet's exiled religious and political leader at the old Royal Commonwealth Society in London. Generously, the Asia Committee of Friends Service Committee, as I believe it then was called, decided that I should go on their behalf. The Dalai Lama disconcertingly arrived in a huge black

Daimler, of the kind used for weddings and funerals. But he dispelled all formality when he bounded into the room in which dignitaries from varied British faith groups were assembled. Maybe because I was incongruously young and slightly shabby, I was introduced first. He stretched out his hand which I took in mine, but my carefully prepared question about serfdom and Tibetan Buddhism just froze in my gullet. Instead, as if moved by some force outside my being, I found myself silently tickling the palm of the Dalai Lama with my index finger. He let out a shriek of surprised delight and was still giggling furiously in his characteristic way as he moved on to the next person. Mortified, I slunk out discreetly as soon as I could.

Perhaps subconsciously I realised that my unvoiced question was only the tip of the iceberg as far as my uncomfortable queries about Buddhism were concerned. For the more I thought about it, the more the idea of enlightenment as a personal liberation from suffering struck me as being somewhat selfish. Besides, was not the Buddhist view of life unduly pessimistic? Why did one need to escape from life? Of course, there were plenty of terrible things in the world, including the Vietnam War. But there was so much that was beautiful and life-affirming. I returned to my books, in the hope of finding an answer.

The Buddha himself saw three realities that left him feeling glum: sickness, old age and death. All three seemed to be inescapable, and in a world in which there was no National Health Service or social security, their impact could indeed be devastating. Hence the stress on suffering. But the prospect of what life held in store was made far worse, as I was beginning to realise, by the Buddhist belief in reincarnation and transmigration. One would not just go through one pattern of birth, sickness, old age and death, but would do so repeatedly, tied to the wheel of life, unless one managed to get off by achieving Nirvana. That might take thousands of years, or could in fact go on for ever. Put that way, the prospect did seem unappetising. Apparently one could have some say in the nature of one's future existence, according to what sort of life one led each time. This meant not only what station in human life one might be born into (particularly important in the Indian context), but even what sort of creature one might be. I began to speculate, in ways of which my university tutor did not approve, about what I would have to do to ensure that I was born as a golden retriever next time round. Behind the flippancy (and a genuine love of dogs) was a growing suspicion that the Buddhism that I had once thought might hold some real promise for me might be a load of old codswallop, just like the Anglican liturgy that I had so decisively rejected before.

The saving grace was the meditation that was part and parcel of the Buddhist experience, even in the academic context. In common with other religions that were born in India, Buddhism for the serious initiate involves a great deal of meditation, though the Buddha was quite clear that meditation should be seen as a tool, not as an end in itself. Meditation can lead to a heightened state of awareness. And although that state is not permanent, I personally challenged the assertion made by some Buddhist commentators that it leaves the individual fundamentally unchanged. I eschewed some of the more formulaic approaches to meditation favoured by some Buddhist sects, and never even attempted to get my cumbersome body into the lotus position. But sitting straight-backed, my arms relaxed and my eyes focussed on some object, until a transformation of my perception and sense of being began to take place, I began to experience a tranquillity and a sense of proportion that could be regenerated on other occasions. Moreover, some trace of it remained with me long after a session of meditation was finished.

The thing was, though, that I found this state easier to access in silence, rather than against a backdrop of ritualistic chanting or bells or the foghorn pipes that I encountered in Lhasa when I eventually got to Tibet, long after graduating from university. For the true Buddhist seeker, such sounds should be an aid to enlightenment, whereas to me they proved to be a distraction. Probably that is why in the end I decided to throw in my lot with the Quakers, rather than becoming a Buddhist.

I spent many years struggling with Chinese texts, and travelled extensively in Buddhist lands. And there were moments – such as coming across a group of monks preparing tea among the ruins of Angkor Wat in Cambodia – when I felt a joyous intuition of spirituality as well as of beauty. But at the end of the day, having caught just the tiniest glimpse of the Buddha, far in the distance, I crossed the road and passed by on the other side.

**The Author**

Jonathan Fryer is a member of the Ratcliff and Barking Monthly Meeting of the Religious Society of Friends. He is a writer and broadcaster familiar to listeners to BBC Radio 4's *From Our Own Correspondent*. He is the author of ten non-fiction books and lectures part time at London University's School of Oriental and African Studies (SOAS).

# Some Aspects of Islam

## Ihsan R. Rasmy

I WAS BORN IN the biblical town of Sidon, Lebanon and although my father prayed and fasted during Ramadan his Sufi spirit saw no harm in leaving his children in the care of a Christian nanny or sending them to a Quaker school. This policy of our parents which included my mother spending the summer vacations with the family of our Christian nanny in the Lebanese mountains had a profound effect on our upbringing. We grew up to ignore the religious walls which were to us invisible and to consider all around us, whether Christian or Muslim, as our brothers and sisters.

At a later date we moved to Palestine where my father allowed me to enrol at a Franciscan College where the Fathers and Friars were examples of tolerance and love. My education was cemented in the Faculty of Law at the University of Cairo where we studied Islamic Law and Jurisprudence in depth. There we were taught Islam and its Shari'a by two Sheikhs whose turbans covered heads as wide as the sky above. Christian girls wearing their crosses showed their love for the lectures of those two Sheikhs by attending every one of them though they missed others. Here the spirit of Sufism about which I had read when I was twelve years old was confirmed to me as I looked on Islam as a universal religion which embraced Judaism and Christianity.

The history of Islam started with Muhammad who from a young age was impressed by the two faiths, Judaism and Christianity, which dominated the Near East at that time. He was horrified by the state of the Arabs at that era in history for they were engaged in perpetual warfare, had no social code and, worst of all, worshipped idols. He found himself retreating to a cave near Mecca thinking about the messy state of his tribe. It was in that cave that he received the divine message from the angel Gabriel that he was to preach the essence of the two faiths, namely the worship of the one and only God or Allah, the God of Abraham.

Although he was inspired to shape his new religion to suit the legitimate needs of the Arabs, the Meccans resisted his message and fought him bitterly, forcing him to flee to Yahtreb (Medina). There, he was dismayed that the community of Jews and Christians turned against him inspiring the saying from the Qu'ran:

*O people of the Book, do you hate and despise us because we believe in God and in our scripture as well as yours?*

Little by little, with the help of God, Muhammad gained the upper hand. With a small number of followers he vanquished the tribe of Quraish and the Meccans. After that, the flow of Arabs into his new religion accelerated, peace was established with the Qu'ranic verse:

*The faithful servants of the Beneficent are they who walk modestly upon the earth and when the foolish ones address them they answer* **Peace be upon you!**

Throughout the ages Muslims have saluted a passing stranger with these words.

The peaceful message of Islam is emphasised by Muhammed in his saying:

*Shall I inform you of an act better than praying and fasting? It is making peace with another, for enmity and malice tear up heavenly rewards by the roots. A man's true wealth is the amount of good he does in his life.*

Today this peaceful message of Islam has got buried under political and tribal upheavals. The violence of a minority of extremist Muslims, reinforced by stereotype television images of bearded Muslims and women in tent like coverings fan the flames of prejudice.

Islam is not a homogeneous religion but one that lives today in different and diverse cultures, aspects of which have infiltrated Islam. It would be wrong, therefore, to assume that outward exhibitionist forms of piety or the violent action of some Muslims reflect the true teaching of Islam. In her book *Muhammad* Karen Armstrong states:

> *It is really impossible to generalise about the rise of this more radical form of this religion. It not only differs from country to country, but from town to town and village to village. But in each case the type of Islam is entirely different and idiosyncratic and is deeply affected by local traditions that are not specially religious.*
>
> *A clear example of stereotyping Islam is the common assumption that Islam practised in Saudi Arabia is the most authentic form of this faith. But Wahhabism is only an Islamic sect, it developed in the eighteenth century and was similar to the Christian Puritan sect, and it is a mistake to view either sect as normative of their religion.*

In her book *Islam* she says:

> *Western people often assume that Islam is a violent materialistic faith which imposed itself on its subject people at sword point. This is an inaccurate interpretation of the Muslim wars of expansion. There was nothing religious about these campaigns.*

The two great wars in 20th century Europe had nothing to do with Christianity any more than the past wars of Arab expansion and the violence today have anything to do with Islam.

Some critics of the Qu'ran and promoters of hostility between Christianity and Islam point out a few verses in the Qu'ran which appear to contradict Qu'ranic tolerance but such people, regrettably some Muslims among them, build their assumption on erroneously translated texts nor do they take into account the circumstances in which the text was revealed. Muhammad, the supreme interpreter of the Qu'ran, enshrined the attitude of Islam towards Christianity in a Charter dated 627 AD given to the Christians of Arabia. He himself undertook and enjoined his followers to protect the Christians and their churches, monasteries and the residencies of their priests, even exhorting Muslims to help Christians with the repair of their churches if required.

The universality of the message of Islam is evident from the Qu'ranic verses, one of which decrees:

*Say we believe in God and the revelation given to us, and to Abraham, Ishmael, Isaac, Jacob and the Tribes. We believe in what was given to Moses and to Jesus, and all the other Prophets from their Lord. We make no distinction between any of them and to God we submit ourselves.*

A more inclusive text reads:

*All who commit themselves to God and do good shall be rewarded by their Lord.*

Matthew Fox, described as one of the important religious thinkers and teachers of our time formerly a member of the Dominican order, and at present an Episcopalian priest in California, wrote in his book *One River, Many Wells*:

*Islam considers the acceptance of anterior prophets as a necessary article of faith and asserts quite vigorously the universality of revelation. No other sacred text speaks as much and as openly of the universality of religion as the Qu'ran.*

The Quakers of Christianity must be mentioned in this context for they also point to the universality of Jesus' Christianity.

As far as the general status of women and their treatment within Islam is concerned, contrary to popular belief in the West that Muslims treat their women woefully, women were respected and loved by Muhammad. It is he who said:

*Paradise is under the feet of mothers.*

When after twenty six years of marriage to Khadija she died, he married Aisha, daughter of Abu-Bakr, the first Caliph and one of his first disciples. He then took further wives – old widows who were left destitute when their husbands were killed during the persecution of the Muslims by the Arabs of Quraish. According to the Arab code of the time marriage was the only way in which Muhammad could offer these women protection. The Qu'ran intended to put an end to the polygamy practised by Arabs before Muhammad:

*Ye may marry of the women who please you two, three or four but if ye fear that ye cannot observe equity between them, then espouse only one. And ye will never be able to be equitable and just between them, no matter how much ye may strive to do so.*

It may be surmised, therefore, that the direction was clearly towards monogamy and to quote Matthew Fox again:

*The ideal relationship in the Qu'ran is monogamy....... People are equal as the teeth of a comb. There is no preference of an Arab over a non-Arab, or of a white person over a non-white, or of a male over a female, except in their piety.*

The Qu'ran gives equality to women in social activities, education, voting, vocation and gave them the right to inheritance.

Fahlalla Haeri, a Muslim scholar, wrote in his book *Islam* that

*Muslim women are discouraged from being excessively concerned with personal beauty yet it is permitted to have as fine and varied a wardrobe as one likes. Neither the Qu'ran nor the Prophet ordered tent-like clothing, burqas or the like. These oppressive costumes were an ethnic and cultural invention.*

Such clothing found its way into the wardrobe of some Muslim women in some Muslim countries after the Khomeini revolution in Iran. The veil worn today in some areas of the Muslim world has nothing to do with the teaching of Islam but is a remnant of the custom of veiling women which prevailed in Persia and Christian Byzantium where women were marginalized. So the dress that some Muslim women have adopted today has nothing to do with their religion although they may think otherwise.

Sufis have explained the varied practices of Islam and other religions by likening religion to a chameleon, coloured by the grounds on which it runs. They looked at the core of Islam and concluded that it is unified with other religions in its ideals. Like Quakers, Sufis answer to that of God in everyone, believing that the spark of God resides in all human beings. The main stem of Islam combines all previous religions of God which is why Rumi said:

*Call me a Jew – I am one; call me a Christian – I am one; and call me a Muslim – I am one.*

The Qu'ran says about the diversity of faith:

*We have given you the Book (Qu'ran) which confirms the scriptures that came before it; and for each of you We have ordained a law and a way to follow. Had God wanted to create you all as a single community He could have done so, but it is His will to test you, so compete in being the first to do acts of goodness and to Him you will all return and He will resolve your disputes.*

Wouldn't it be wonderful to have all humanity following this example? I think it is the Quaker way.

It is easy, therefore, to understand why Rumi said:

*The lamps are many but the Light is the same. It comes from beyond. If thou keep looking at the lamp thou art lost for thence arises the appearance of number and plurality. Fix thy gaze upon the Light and thou art delivered from dualism inherent in the finite body.*

Ibn El-Arabi, that other great Sufi, said:

*Do not attach yourself to a particular creed or religion exclusively so that you disbelieve in all the rest, otherwise you will lose much good; nay, you will fail to recognise the real truth of the matter. God the Omnipresent and Omnipotent is not limited by any one creed. Wheresoever you turn, there is the face of God..*

Isn't it absurd to think that each religion has a separate God competing with others for ascendancy and number of followers? It is sad that some Muslims think their God is the genuine one, while in the same dogmatic way some Christians will insist that the great prophet and teacher Jesus Christ was none other than God himself. But even in face of such dogmatism with which he cannot agree, the Sufi feels free to extend the hand of love and friendship to the Christian, reminding him that perhaps we are all travelling along different paths that will lead us to the same destination, the Throne of God or Allah. That, too, is the Quaker way but Sufis and Quakers, however much they may be on the right path, are still in the minority in the world.

Religions progress and regress with the progress and regression of humanity so it is wrong to judge a religion by the state of its adherents at any particular time. Towards the end of the 19th century Islam was not subject to the present day controversy. Albert Hourani, a Syrian Christian who was an Emeritus Fellow of St Antony's College and Honorary Fellow of Magdalen College, Oxford, wrote in his book about Ignaz Goldziher, a Hungarian Jewish theologian who said that Judaism was the pulse beat of his life. This Jew went to live in the Near East towards the end of the nineteenth century where he met Muslim scholars and divines. He gained permission to attend Al-Azhar, the centre of Islamic learning and wrote afterwards in his diary:

*This was the best period of my life. Life lived in the true spirit of Islam can be an ethically impeccable life, demanding compassion for God's creatures, honesty in one's dealings, love, loyalty and suppression of all selfish impulses.*

Such was the Islam of yesteryear.

A well know Sufi saint called Abu Said Ibn Abi-El-Khayr, summarised Sufism in the saying:

> *The perfect mystic is not an ecstatic devotee lost in contemplation of Oneness, nor a saintly recluse shunning all commerce with mankind, but the true saint goes in and out amongst the people and eats and sleeps with them and buys and sells in the market and marries and takes part in social intercourse and never forgets God for a single moment.*

Another great Sufi, Muhyiddin Ibn El-Arabi, advised:

> *Do not attach yourself to a particular creed or religion so exclusively that you disbelieve in all the rest ... Otherwise you will lose much good. God the omnipotent, the omnipresent, is not limited by one religion or creed. Wherever you turn, there is the face of God.*

I do not follow the religion of Islam so exclusively that I disbelieve in all the rest. Islam requires me to believe in all the anterior pristine religions, and as the principal belief of Quakers is that of God in everyone I find it easy to associate myself with them, and they with me. My wife is a Quaker. Other Quakers in our Meeting appreciate the sayings of the Sufi Rumi and one has visited his shrine in Turkey.

A Sufi saying is that:

> *Religion is like a chameleon: it is coloured by the grounds on which it runs.*

There are some non-authentic religious colours prevailing in the world today professed by people intending to distinguish their beliefs from all others with the consequence of sowing division and even violence. If asked about my religion, I say there is only one: the religion of the living God. Ralph Waldo Trine wrote about the unifying principles of all religions:

> *The great fundamental principles of all religions are the same. They differ only in the various degrees of unfoldment of people.*

All Sufis attempt to travel the path of love which is the only path humanity should travel if it wishes to live in peace and harmony, and do away with the violence and conflict which we see around us today. Muhammad said that making peace between one another is better than praying or fasting. In their Peace Testimony Quakers attempt to give substance to the words of Jesus:

> *Blessed are the Peace makers for they shall be called the children of God.*

## References

Karen Armstrong (2001) Muhammad: A Biography of the Prophet.
Karen Armstrong (2001) Islam: A Short History.
Albert Hourani (1992) Islam in European Thought.
ed Llewellyn Vaughan-Lee (1995) Travelling the Path of Love – Sayings of Sufi Masters

## The Author

Ihsan R Rasmy was educated in Gaza and Jerusalem and then worked for the British administration in Palestine. He studied law in the university in Cairo and then became an Egyptian diplomat who was posted to the Netherlands, South Africa and Britain. He lost this job during Nasser's regime when it was discovered that his grandfather was not Egyptian as he was born in the North Caucasus! He subsequently acquired British nationality, married an English woman and found a job with the Moroccan embassy in London. A Saudi diplomat helped him financially to set up a printer producing material in the Arabic and Latin scripts, a successful venture lasting ten years until his retirement. His wife is a Friend and he is an Attender at Sidmouth Meeting.

# Across the Indus: Bridges of Faith

## Jennifer Kavanagh

I CAME TO MY faith eight years ago. It was in the wake of trauma, unexpectedly called, that I found against all probability a home with Quakers. I had not known that religion could be like this, not a signing up to a set of beliefs, prescribed prayers and ritual, but a confirmation of a deep self that had always been there. It was a solitary discovery, and I socialised reluctantly, only slowly absorbing the rest of my life into my faith.

I am not a theologian. Although I initially felt attracted to academic exploration, I soon realised that I had to leave behind the cerebral so inculcated by my education and culture. It was my heart and my spirit that would serve me now. I was drawn in parallel to the empowering practical nature of Quakers – it is possible to make a difference – and to the mystic quality of the spiritual life. Through others I was brought for the first time in my life to engagement in social action: first with homeless people, then the immigrant populations in the poorest parts of the East End of London, the practice of microcredit and recently resettlement work in prisons.

From the beginning it has been the writings of mystics that draw me – mystics of all faiths. My parents led the way. My mother, a Russian Jew, became a Kabbalist in her fifties, and my father converted from Anglicanism to the Catholic Church when I was five. Later in life he was much drawn to a monastic way of life, although he was never accepted into an order. His deep exploration and occasional practice of other religions was revealed by the large folder of cuttings on all faiths that we found on his death.

When I came to Quakers and immersed myself in reading not only Quakers but mystic writing of all faiths, I found to my surprise and delight that, despite our different labels, my father, my mother and I were in the same place. Meister Eckhart, Thomas Merton, the Upanishads, *The Tibetan Way of Living and Dying*, F C Happold's *Mysticism* – all were for us a rich seam – a seam explored by Aldous Huxley's *The Perennial Philosophy* – one of the most influential spiritual books in my life. I should say that all this reading was not on a theoretical level: rather a *lectio divina*, a reading with the heart. Like Simone Weil, I am obedient in my reading, devouring only what I am hungry for.

About five years ago, I was introduced to the writings of Bede Griffiths, the Benedictine monk from Prinknash, who went to live in India and developed one of the first Christian ashrams in India, Saccidananda Santivanam, in Tamil Nadu. In his writings he went beyond the constraints of one faith, beyond labels, a coming together of East and West, of Christianity and Hinduism, that found echoes in my soul, a confirmation of the commonality of all faiths.

I am aware that such an approach lays itself open to the accusation of eclecticism, a pick'n mix approach to religion, taking the best from each. This seems to me a shallow accusation, a misunderstanding of the profound truths of what Wayne Teasdale has termed interspirituality: to drink from the pool of human wisdom, to understand that there is one God with many approaches and that at the mystic core we are one – this seems to me part of the indivisible truth that we reach for.

I had always wanted to go to India, but had held off until I could be there for a long stretch of time; in fact, I did not go until I was ready. When I arrived, in 2001, I had a confused idea about Hinduism. At one level, I was persuaded by the view of Charles Elliott:

> *More than other religions, Hinduism appeals to the soul's immediate knowledge and experience of God. The possibility and truth of this experience is hardly questioned in India, and the task of religion is to bring it about* (quoted in Spencer, 18).

At another level was the multiplicity of gods: Ganesh and Vishnu, Kali and Hanuman, brightly coloured idols before which people worship, give obeisance; a polytheistic faith verging on the superstitious.

For three months my then partner and I visited temples, meditated, received *puja*, and talked to *saddhus*. We read deeply, and stayed with Hindu families, and gradually we came to a greater understanding of the faith. We were keen, of course, to spend time at Santivanam: the ashram of Bede Griffiths. Without the presence of Father Bede, the ashram does not have the same weight of spiritual experience and understanding, but it still stands as a remarkable blending of India and the West, a combination of Benedictine monastery and Hindu temple. The open-sided church is itself in the style of a temple topped by Christian figures rather than Hindu gods; the monks wear the saffron of Hindu holy men; the worship is a combination of a Christian service including psalms and prayers (in Tamil) and Eucharist interspersed with meditation; the way of life is simple, sitting on the ground to eat with the right hand, in silence. For me, being there, among monks and pilgrims in a woodland setting, was what was important: the sound of a dry leaf hitting the ground more significant than structured Christian services, which I in any country find uncomfortable and on the whole avoid.

At Santivanam, one of the nuns lent me the journals of Abhishiktananda, a French monk who was the predecessor of Father Bede and the co-founder of the ashram. His writing filled me with excitement and delight. His life's work had been to build a bridge between Christianity and Hinduism; living mainly in a cave in the Himalayas, he wrote and taught extensively. What moved me then and in the letters which I have since read, was the account of his struggles in the early days, struggles to which anyone on a spiritual path could relate.

At the suggestion of other pilgrims, from Santivanam we moved on to Hindu ashrams in the south and east of the country. I found ritual difficult, and on the whole abstained, except when it would have been discourteous to do so. It was refreshing to remind myself of Abhishiktananda:

> *To fulfil the ultimate demands of his religion, the Hindu leaves behind all the rites and formulas of his religion* (Stuart 93).

As we travelled on, we found ourselves in a liberal universalist Hindu tradition that included such figures as Ramakrishna, whose centre we visited in Delhi, and his disciple, Vivekenanda, and some of my confusion was laid to rest. Vivekananda, in the famous *Paper on Hinduism* given in his address to the Parliament of Religions, held in Chicago in 1893, said:

> *There is no polytheism in India...External worship, material worship, say the scriptures, is the lowest stage...the attempt of undeveloped minds to grasp high spiritual truths.*
>
> *...The Hindus have discovered that the absolute can only be realised, or thought of, or stated, through the relative, and the images, crosses, crescents are simply so many symbols – so many pegs to hang spiritual ideas on. It is not that this help is necessary for everyone, but those that do not need it have no right to say that it is wrong. Nor is it compulsory in Hinduism.* (Vivekananda, 44-6).

Polytheism had been rejected too by the influential Brahmo Samaj (the Society of God), founded in 1828 by a Bengali Brahmin, Ram Mohan Roy, and taken up by the father of the poet Rabindranath Tagore. Like early Quakers, they felt they were reverting to an earlier, purer stage of their religion. The movement emphasised the importance of the formless universal spirit: the monotheistic basis of Hinduism, and its links with other faiths. It was good to understand that

Vishnu, Kali, or Ganesh, as well as the Christian saints and angels, could be seen as entry points to the deeper mystical faith beyond.

The ibiblio.org website defines Hinduism as:

*Historically Hinduism has developed over about 4,000 years and has no single founder or creed. Rather, it consists of a vast variety of beliefs and practices. Organisation is minimal and hierarchy non-existent. In its diversity, Hinduism hardly fits most Western definitions of religion, rather, it suggests commitment to or respect for an ideal way of life, known as Dharma.\**

*Hinduism is a vast and profound religion. It worships one supreme Reality (called by many names), teaches that all souls ultimately realise truth. There is no eternal hell or damnation. It accepts all genuine spiritual paths, from pure monism (God alone exists) to theistic dualism (when shall I know His Grace?) Each soul is free to find his own way, whether by devotion, austerity, meditation, yoga, or selfless service.*

Easy from this to see its attraction for a Quaker. It goes on:

*Love, non-violence, good conduct, and the law of Dharma define the Hindu path. Hinduism is a mystical religion, leading to the truth within, finally reaching the pinnacle of consciousness where man and God are one.*

It is in the bits in between that the problems arise for me: among them the importance of the guru/disciple relationship, the central tenets of reincarnation and karma, and the caste system.

If the worship of statues worried me, the obeisance to gurus, human beings both living and dead, disturbed me more

---

\* A better definition, taken from Manu, the foremost lawgiver of the Hindus, is 'that by which a thing maintains itself in being and without which it would cease to be the thing it is.' For mankind it is the quest for spirituality.

deeply. At the shrines of Sri Aurobindo and his disciple, The Mother, in Pondicherry, and that of Sri Ramana Maharishi at Tiruvannamalai, followers worshipped and gave offerings in their hundreds. The chatter and busyness at Tiruvannamalai was distracting, and ironic, since Sri Ramana himself preferred to communicate through the power of silence, a silence so profound that it stilled the minds of those who came to visit him. Only in the small whitewashed cave where he lived did that silence linger, and in a few moments of a home movie that I have seen recently, in which he looks, for several minutes, quite unblinking, at the camera.

Many years ago, another visitor, disturbed by this worship of the then living Mother, wrote to her and asked *Mother, are you God? Yes*, she replied, *and so are you.*

The guru/disciple relationship, demanding complete obedience, is not one that has an attraction for an independent-minded Quaker. The transmission of wisdom through generations in this way is central to many of the world's faiths, of course, and as an inner call rather than as an external imposition has to be taken seriously. Abhishiktananda says that guru and disciple are like two poles of a magnet. When the disciple is ready, the guru appears. But he refines that position:

*For the Vedantin there is only one guru, the one who shines, not-born in the depth of the heart. The external guru is only the temporary form taken by the essential guru to make himself recognised, and at the moment of that recognition there is no longer either guru or disciple...The Christian guru [individual in the Church] is never anything but the manifestation of the Lord.* (Stuart, 238).

Elsewhere he admits that there is an

*Advaitic [non-dualistic] insight which allows no intermediary in the quest for the Absolute.* (Stuart, 83).

That is my position: no intermediaries are needed in that quest, though the path is sometimes lonely, and sometimes I find myself hankering for a guide.

Quakers have a different answer, and that difference is fundamental. Communal worship is not a major part of Hindu life – practice is dependent on personal wishes, and *puja* is usually individual. For Quakers communal worship is the one immutable feature – you cannot hold a Meeting for Worship on your own – and it is in that meeting of equals, spiritual companions not teacher and pupil, that spiritual experience is shared. In *The Power of Prayer* Swami Swahananda wrote:

*Group prayer is not an aggregate but a symphony.*

He might have been talking of a Meeting for Worship.

Not having experienced anything to tell me otherwise, I have an open mind about an afterlife, and it does not exercise me greatly. Although I can see the scientific logic of reincarnation, it seems to me unlikely to take a bodily form. I expressed this view recently to a young man of Hindu/Jain parentage, living in this country. He said he had taken the same view but of late had felt within himself the truth of reincarnation – as part of the interconnectedness of all things, and the continuance of more than molecules. It suddenly made sense.

I am uneasy with the concept of karma; it seems among other things to be an easy way of explaining away the inequalities of birth (why do we imagine that we can understand everything?), but there have also been many misunderstandings about it, suggestions that it leads to passivity and fatalism. The opposite could be said to be true: that it is about taking responsibility for your life, how you live now will affect your future lives. The law of cause and effect is not immutable: God's mercy is always available. The notion of grace is important in Hinduism, but man must be prepared to receive it.

The profound social impact of religious beliefs and practices that so impresses visitors to India bears with it its own danger. A false interpretation, a corruption, will seep deep into the roots of the country, and be hard to eradicate. The caste system is a case in point. Life tasks according to four divisions of humanity are to be found in the early scriptures, and the concept lies deep in the Indian consciousness. But the original divisions, however arbitrary and rigid they may seem, were not originally made according to heredity but to stages of spiritual maturity. Crucially, untouchability was not originally part of the concept, although later distortions have led to widespread abuse and misery. In modern times the caste system has been on the wane. Arya Samaj, founded in 1875, worked for its abolition as well as other social reforms. Vivekananda in his rejection of exclusion echoes Christ's teaching:

> *Where should you go to seek for God? Are not all the poor, the miserable, the weak, good? Why not worship them first? Why go to dig a well on the shores of the Ganges? Let these people be your God – think of them, work for them, pray for them incessantly. The Lord will show you the way.* (quoted in Suda, 130).

In persuading his brother disciples to give up their peaceful meditation and religious individualism and do social service, he was reverting to the ancient tenets of Hinduism. In the Bhagavad Gita, we hear that:

> *The secret of action, says the Lord to Arjuna, lies in doing it as an offering to God, in the spirit of surrender to Him...*
>
> *The more a person is united with God, the less he is attached to the world...This however, does not mean withdrawal from the world and retirement to the seclusion of a hermitage in a forest...the Gita wants us to be actively engaged in the discharge of our duties but in a spirit of detachment...renunciation of the fruit of action but not of the act itself.* (Suda, 71).

Of one mind with William Penn here:

> *True godliness don't turn men out of the world but enables them to live better in it and excites their endeavours to mend it.* (QFP, 23.02)

It was by this tradition of service as worship that we were so forcibly struck as we travelled round India. At ISARA, a small NGO in the eastern state of Orissa, young men and women work with untouchables and hill tribe people – the outcasts of society. Some of the workers are Brahmins, many graduates; all bed down on the floor of their office, wash from buckets in the yard, and work in the toughest of conditions – for the love of God and their fellow beings. At the Chinmaya Tapovan Trust, a large NGO near Dharamsala in the North-West, volunteers and modestly paid workers devote themselves to work in hundreds of neighbouring villages. Founded by Swami Chinmayananda (Guru Dev), the charity is run devotionally by his disciple, the magnificent Kshama Metre. For her and those who work for her, worship is service, contemplation is in action. All work in all the projects starts with prayer and with devotional ritual to Guru Dev. The greeting in the organisation is Hare Om (the word of the Lord). Unexpectedly, one of the books Kshama gave me as a parting present: *On the Path, Preparing for the Spiritual Quest*, contains essays by Thomas Merton and Jacob Boehme, and quotes from Guru Nanak, the Koran, the Buddha and a Christian saint, Kshama. A contemplative Hindu, is open to Light from whatever source it may come.

The broad range of Hindu practice was shown by the people with whom we stayed: for one family, regular visits to the temple and daily worship in the home were essential, with Sarasvati, the goddess of the arts and knowledge, as their household goddess. Another, Kamla, is a non-practising Hindu, but nonetheless felt impelled to leave the comfort of teaching at one of India's elite schools to start up a charity school in a provincial town in Haryana Province, and live in a house much smaller and with very basic facilities. She says she does not feel she has a choice; that although she does not practise or talk about religion, she feels called by something outside herself. As a scientist she does not have much time for gurus who are worshipped for their magic tricks and do not appear to have anything new to say. The attraction of Hinduism for her is that it enables individuals to worship in the way they think best, that it does not dictate practices but encourages choice. Like many Quakers and other Hindus that we met, she feels that the way of life is what matters.

It is hard to discern what it is in my experience of Hinduism that has influenced me, that has deepened my faith; all is so entwined, rooted now. Perhaps I can pick out the threads of universality, non-duality, the one God of all creation, so well described too by Meister Eckhart: *Every creature is a word of God,* and tolerance. In participating, albeit reluctantly, in Hindu ritual I have learnt to be tolerant of something alien to me, to value the spiritual comradeship of entering into another practice without letting go of my right to abstain (as I do with hymns that do not speak my truth). My concept of simplicity has deepened by seeing with how little people in India are content. My letting go is influenced by the Hindu view of the latter stages in life, from forest hermit at about the age of fifty to older sannyasins, free from every bond, leaving home as mendicants and aiming for union with the divine.

As with Quakerism, the attractions of Hinduism for me are the parallel strands of the practical and the mystical. The mysticism in the Upanishads – in the lives of swamis, gurus and sannyasi, has drawn millions to the shores of India; in turn the devotion of millions of Hindus have brought them to work for others, to express their faith in love towards those less fortunate than themselves, to express their worship in service.

It should be said that the name Hinduism is an artificial one, its literal meaning referring to the people beyond the Indus; some feel a more exact term might be Vedantism. But that is to separate the faith from the culture, and that is exactly to miss the point about the greatness, the breadth of the experience of India. The two are inextricably connected. I had never understood why people felt they had to go to India to find their spiritual identities; I had always thought it more appropriate to find a faith that related to their own culture. What I had not understood before coming to India was that people do not necessarily come to learn about another faith – Vedantism – but rather to inhale the spiritual oxygen, to experience India in all its richness, both the roots *and* the manifestations of faith. And that has perhaps been the greatest influence on me: the way Hinduism demonstrates that it is possible for the religious life of a nation to be so embedded in the culture of its citizens that all religious acts – bathing in the Ganges or sending flowers to sail down it, blowing the conch shell at sunset – are viewed as intrinsic parts of daily life.

A sense of community, interconnectedness, is expressed in many ways in India – in the closeness of families, in respect for all living creatures, indeed in the doctrine of reincarnation. A spiritual path is solitary, unique, but a faith community provides a grounding, a human context. Despite a tendency to go it alone, I now belong to faith communities such as the Bede Griffiths Sangha and The Catherine Collective (a group of women of various faiths with whom I retreat every year). I also have looser connections with the Alister Hardy Association and the Gandhi Foundation. But my principal spiritual community is the Religious Society of Friends. My path, my faith, is in the context of Quakers, the practice of it according to the manner of Quakers, my way of life in keeping with Quakers' belief. Where Hinduism meets that spirit, that way of life, I feel a real connection; as with Christianity, at the level of ritual or religion it has little interest for me. Gandhi asked whether Quakers would be prepared to *recognise that it is as natural for a Hindu to grow into a Friend as it is for a Christian...* Many of us do. I am not a Hindu, or indeed a Christian, although I am enriched by both traditions. The only label that I accept is Friend, and I delight in the richness that that encompasses.

I give the last word to Vivekananda:

*If there is ever to be a universal religion, it must be one which will have no location in place or time, which will be infinite like the God it will preach, and whose sun will shine upon the followers of Krishna and of Christ, on saints and sinners alike; which will not be Brahminic or Buddhistic, Christian or Mohammedan, but the sum total of all these, and still have infinite space for development...It will be a religion which will have no place for persecution or intolerance in its polity, which will recognise divinity in every man and woman, and whose whole scope, whose whole force, will be centred in aiding humanity to realise its own true, divine nature. Offer such a religion, and all the nations will follow you.* (Vivekananda, 48-9)

## References

Mascaro, Juan (trans), *The Upanishads*, Penguin, 1965.
Quaker Faith & Practice: the book of Christian Discipline of the Yearly Meeting of the Religious Society of Friends (Quakers) in Britain, 1995.
Spencer, Sidney, *Mysticism in World Religion*, Penguin, 1963.
Stuart, James, *Swami Abhishiktananda: His Life Told Through His Letters*, Delhi: ISPCK, 1995.
Suda, J.P., *Religions in India*, Delhi: Sterling, 1978.
Vivekananda, Swami, *Chicago Addresses*, Kolkata: Advaita Ashram, 2001.

## The Author

Jennifer Kavanagh was born in London and is Jewish by birth, Anglican by upbringing. She became a Quaker in 1996. After nearly thirty years in publishing she sold her literary agency and began work in the community. She went round the world in 2001/2, and has taken up project work in the fields of microcredit, conflict resolution and prison reform. Her first book, *Call of the Bell Bird*, was published in 2004. She is working on another on living a contemplative and engaged life in the world. Jennifer has two children, is a trained singer and much involved in Quaker outreach.

# Some Aspects of Hinduism

## Hallam Tennyson

MY WIFE AND I went to India in 1946 to work on a project of village development with funds provided by the American Quakers. The area chosen was seventy miles south east of Calcutta, an area which had suffered disastrously in the 1942 famine. I became fairly proficient in the Bengali language, which I still regard as particularly beautiful, and the fact that I could talk to the villagers evoked an overwhelming outpouring of affection and trust: the result of this was that I developed a very special sympathy with the Hindu background from which most of the villagers sprang.

Hinduism is the oldest of the world's great religions. It is at the same time the simplest and the most complex, the subtlest and the most primitive, the most basic and the most highly developed. Make one statement about it and the opposite can immediately be invoked.

For the Westerner the caste system within Hinduism is a big problem. The Sanskrit is *Varna* which also means colour. The system was imposed by the conquering Aryans in about 1200 BC when they subjugated the dark skinned native Dravidians whom they pushed southwards. They were given a lowly social role as servants and street cleaners. South Indians are notably darker skinned to this day. The priestly caste of Brahmins remain much fairer skinned.

The central tenets of Hinduism are most succinctly set out in the *Bhagavad Gita* or *Holy Song.*. It is supposedly spoken by Krishna to the Prince Arjuna before a great battle. This fascinating text puts the doctrines of the *Upanishads* within an existential experience of a moral and political dilemma. Is one justified in slaying to establish righteousness? How can we achieve balance and enlightenment in a world of danger and insecurity? The *Gita* is rightly regarded as one of the most rational and convincing of religious texts. It is devoid of dogma or metaphysics and there is hardly a word that an agnostic, or even an atheist, would find difficult to accept. We must act in a positive and selfless fashion, not only to avoid the cycle of rebirths, but also because it is the surest way to social justice and human happiness.

Lacking central doctrinal control, Hinduism has developed a vast number of cults and sects. The most common is that of the Vaishnavites the followers of Vishnu who came to earth in the form of Krishna. It is Krishna who propounded the Bhagavad Gita. But he is no solemn preacher: he led a very human life in Northern India as a cowherd. He was supposed to have flirted outrageously with the milkmaids. This happy legend is entertaining and enchanting and his devoted followers travel the countryside singing romantic and touching songs about his exploits. The singers, mostly men, dressed as Radha, the leading milkmaid, perform on trains and in bazaars. Noone seems perturbed about the likelihood of their unusual sexual activities. The Khumb Mela, which takes place every four years at Krishna's alleged birth place, attracts upwards of thirty million people. It is the largest gathering in the world.

Another cult, not so endearing, is the worship of Kali, the Goddess of Destruction, a black lady left over from the Dravidian past. She is still thought to be worshipped with human sacrifice although this was outlawed a hundred and fifty years ago. She holds an upraised sword, the severed head of her consort, as well as various other symbols of female power. In spite of her fearsome nature Kali inspires simple devotion as the Divine Mother. Kali hymns, or Kirtan, written by devotees over many centuries, are among India's most beautiful religious lyrics. Another popular deity is Ganesh, the Elephant God, patron of travellers. No long distance bus or lorry journey would be thought safe without his comic pot-bellied figure dangling from the dashboard.

How far are these symbolic figures regarded as real? Veneration involves suspension of disbelief: metaphor within Hinduism is indeed all pervading. The multiplicity of symbols has the effect of making every aspect of human life a vehicle for the Divine. Virtue resides in linking these symbols to an inner world. It is perhaps significant that Gandhi's favourite Christian hymn was the Evangelical

*A servant with this clause makes drudgery divine*
*Who sweeps a room as by Thy laws making the action Thine*

To the horror of missionaries sex in Hinduism still has the importance once accorded in Greece to the famous Mysteries. Copulation is an expression of the life force that is inherent in all human existence. Great temples in Southern India have towers in which naked human figures writhe upwards in sexual ecstasy. Yet at the same time in ordinary life a sexual code is enforced which seems to us positively Victorian. In Bollywood movies it is exceptional to see more than a chaste kiss on the forehead exchanged between lovers.

Puja, or worship, whether in temple or in open fields, celebrates the Divine Spirit in all things. Every natural phenomenon contains this spirit: among trees the Peepul, among animals primarily the Monkey, among rivers the Brahmaputre, among mountains the Kailash. These traditional symbols are subject to no controlling centre, they can spring up spontaneously anywhere: a sort of glorified animism run riot. This is popular Hinduism: funny, touching, astonishing, enjoyed by all. At the top end of the scale is the higher Hinduism believed by Schopenhauer to be the greatest philosophical system ever to be invented by the human mind.

The first of these texts are the *Rig Vedas* celebrating the glorious phenomena of the physical world. They are undatable but probably three to four thousand years old. Out of these developed the *Upanishads,* or secret doctrine, which date from about 1400 BC. These texts discuss the nature of Self, the core of which is held to be the Atman echoed in the German Atem, breath . Yoga, the word is cognate with our word yoke, sets out an exhaustive system of meditation, ascetic practices, and mental control that aims at a coalescence of the individual's identity with the Universal Self. This state is known as *Sat-chit-ananda* – Truth, Knowledge, Bliss. Its achievement leads to release from the cycle of life and reincarnation. In theory all human beings can achieve this condition whatever their background. But in my experience very few people thought that they had achieved it. Those attempting it are called Sanyasins but as they usually retire to the Himalayas it is perhaps not surprising that one does not meet them frequently in ordinary life. But in the countryside one does meet many religious mendicants, soothsayers, singers, yogis, who claim to be striving for religious enlightenment.

The yogis practise an amazing variety of ascetic usages. I was once present at the disinterment of a yogi who had been buried underground for three months with no access to oxygen. His tongue had been forked to enable him to block his nasal passages . He emerged apparently little the worse for wear. This kind of achievement is still by no means uncommon and the control of one's physical being through yogic practices is an important aspect of Hindu culture, one which exerts an enduring fascination on the Western mind.

The norms laid down for ordinary mortals, charity, chastity, and family loyalty, are much the same as those found in all great religions. To carry through successfully the tasks of daily life is a cause for celebration and respect. Birth, marriage, death, are celebrated with unique and imposing ceremonies. It is in this every day world that women, who have always contributed vigorously to Hindu spiritual life, play a pre-eminent role: the mother is all important. My great Indian friend Sachin Chaudhuri, who edited Asia's finest financial weekly, would undertake no new venture unless it had first received his mother's blessing. Many are the Ashrams (monasteries) with the Mother as their spiritual head. Mahatma Gandhi, one of the towering figures of the twentieth century, gave an extraordinarily high status to women among his followers. This resulted in India being the very first country to place women in leading positions in national and international politics.

At the Ramakrishna Centres throughout the world the main Christian and Muslim festivals are celebrated along with the many Hindu holy days. Christ and Mohammed are regarded as great spiritual leaders. On the other hand Hinduism is universally condemned as socially exclusive. The fact that government legislation had to be introduced in order to allow lower castes to enter Hindu temples, a law still widely disregarded, arouses horror in our democratic consciences. What non-Hindus forget is that the Hindu religion belongs as much in the open air as inside the temple. In public worship the lower castes, the various sects, and even the local Muslims, all join together to enjoy a festival of fun. In the villages where I lived the Muslims were expected to provide the music. I am not sure whether this still happens but it was central to my village experience.

Where does modern India stand with regard to re-incarnation? The West used to look upon this as the main tenet of Hinduism. Human beings achieved deliverance through a sequence of gradually improving lives. Re-incarnation is one of the tenets of Buddhism, which the Buddha is said to have adopted when he departed from orthodox Hinduism in about 500 BC. In my experience, Hindus rarely seem influenced by this doctrine. In fact, I do not think I ever once heard it referred to when I lived in the Bengal countryside. A Hindu believes in loyalty, benevolence, tolerance and unselfishness because this is what makes social life bearable, not because such virtues will free him from rebirth.

Modern Hinduism has been affected by its contact with the Christian West. From the time of Raj Mohan Roy at the beginning of the nineteenth century to Mahatma Gandhi who was assassinated in 1947 by a Hindu fanatic opposed to his tolerance of Islam and other religions, the great religious leaders have sought to integrate Hindu teaching with the moral and social values of Christianity. Now the tide has turned and yoga exerts a powerful influence on Western religious attitudes.

This exchange has been fruitful but the core of Hinduism has not been affected by it. The religion has, after all, retained its distinctive ethos over a period of three thousand years. However, recently Hinduism has begun to develop an ugly and uncharacteristic intolerance. It is an ironic reminder that Hindus have never before indulged in a Holy War or attempted enforced conversion on a mass scale. Bali, the only country outside India to be Hindu, was converted by infiltration not by force. It has never accepted the caste system. Will this phase of Indian nationalism pass?

The central doctrine of the Hindu religion lies in the famous phrase *Om-Shanti-Shanti*: hope for universal peace devoid of any suggestion of self-righteousness. This will remain when temporary aberrations have faded.

Certainly my experience of Hinduism at the village level has had a profound effect on my life. The world seen as an embodiment of mysterious and hidden forces gains immeasurably in interest and vitality: the disasters and setbacks that we all endure are accepted as an inevitable part of the terrible beauty of life. I don't believe that Hindus would react to the Tsunami disaster with the words *How could God allow this?* To Hindus *God* is immanent in all creation: we each carry the atman or spirit within us. We must, of course, work to establish peace, prosperity and brotherhood but we will never wholly succeed and, unlike the Psalmist's prophecy, will never *dwell together in unity* for more than a few moments. There will always be *triumph and disaster* and *we have to learn to treat these two impostors just the same*, as Kipling remarked having absorbed much from India.

In the end a religion must be judged from its effect on the workaday world. The trust and affection which Margot, to whom I was married, and I received from the villagers of Bengal had nothing to do with any material benefits that our neighbours might have hoped to gain from us. We were loved and we were never asked for favours. It was a love grounded in Hindu culture. Its effect is still with me nearly sixty years later.

**The Author**

Hallam Tennyson worked for many years in the BBC Radio Drama Department. He was the first producer to sponsor work by Harold Pinter. He has published three books about India: a novel *The Dark Goddess*, a biography of the Indian Saint Vinoba Bhave, *Saint on the March* and an autobiography *The Haunted Mind* in which India features strongly. He still practises the Bengali he learned to speak while in India due to the prevalence of Bengali shopkeepers. At present he is working on a play about Beethoven as well as a personal memoir of Peter Benenson, founder of Amnesty International, with whom he and his wife Margot shared a house for eight years in a successful reproduction of the traditional Bengali joint family.

# A Point of Light: Meeting the Brahma Kumaris

## David Cadman

MANY QUAKERS ARE comfortable in the company of other faiths. Indeed, given our hesitation at imposing religious practice on even our own members, the foibles and peculiarities of others are, if anything, a constant source of interest and, sometimes, fascination.

Nevertheless, the first time that you visit Global Co-operation House in Wembley is an odd experience. Driving through rows of houses in north London, and turning into Pound Lane, a quiet, tree-lined road that runs alongside a large area of allotments, you come upon what, at first, appears to be a suburban office block. However, crossing the pavement and entering the building you find yourself standing in the reception area of what is clearly not an ordinary office. The walls are covered with murals painted in pinks, blues and lime green and the entire staff seem to be women dressed in white saris, some, because of the season, with the addition of a white cardigan. This is the London headquarters of the Brahma Kumaris.

Now you have to readjust the parameters of your expectations. On the one hand you appear to have left what we often call the real world. Indeed, if you arrive on the half hour you are likely to hear the tannoy announcing traffic control – an instruction to stop whatever it is that you are doing and enter a brief period of silence and reflection, before resuming whatever it was that seemed so urgent at the time. On the other hand, it soon becomes clear that this is a place of administration and highly focussed work, the centre of a large organisation. With their global headquarters on Mount Abu, Rajasthan in northern India, the Brahma Kumaris have 5,000 branches in over 80 countries. Indeed, they present themselves as a worldwide Spiritual University, and on Mount Abu they have a lecture hall that can take 20,000 people, and the world's largest solar cooker with a capacity for 60,000 meals a day. What is more, if you spend some time browsing through the bookshop that stands at one side of the reception area, you will see that this is a group of people that is involved not only at the grassroots, with local inter-faith work and with courses and seminars but, most especially, is active globally, working with the United Nations and other governmental initiatives for education, peace and health care.

I have come to meet Dadi Janki, one of the three most senior women of the Brahma Kumaris (or BK, as they are known) and the person responsible for all of their work outside India. I am taken upstairs and along a corridor until I come to a door in front of which is a row of shoes, neatly arranged. I take off my shoes, add them to the row, and go into a comfortable room set about with low armchairs and decorated with pictures that must represent aspects of the teachings of the BK. There are flowers on a table. After a short while, and accompanied by a number of her sisters, all clad in white, Dadi Janki comes into the room to greet me. She is small and elderly but at once I am aware of an inner energy and authority. Indeed, someone once described her as a woman short in stature but taller than any woman I know. Her eyes are especially bright and I am held by them.

She sits, her feet resting on a footstool. We sit, too, and the sisters adjust their saris and cardigans as if to make ready for a discussion of some importance. Although one of the sisters, acting as interpreter, introduces me to Dadi Janki in Hindi, I feel that she needs the translation less than one might at first suppose. And, as in other moments when I have met people who are truly holy – but this may be no more than my own paranoia – I now have an unnerving sense that she can see deep inside me, bringing into the light all of my frailties. There is no hiding place.

I had planned to ask all sorts of sensible questions but now, despite being drawn by Dadi Janki's evident compassion and, indeed, courtesy, I find myself somewhat lost for words. This, however, is not a problem for within no time at all, and without prompting, she has begun to teach on the very matters that speak to my condition, each fragment spoken in Hindi and then translated for me. Often her words are brought to an end with an expression of the eyes and hands that says: Isn't that the way it is?

This is no ordinary woman and at the end of our meeting, before I am plied with all sorts of sweetmeats and gifts, I am offered *drishti*. This is somewhat unsettling. I am invited to sit in silence (all right so far) and look directly into the eyes of Dadi Janki (not so easy – how often do we avoid eye contact). But not wishing to offend, and conscious that this is an important gift, I surrender. Her eyes are filled with deep compassion. They are a window into another world. And as each moment passes my initial reserve eases and I find myself resting in her gaze, allowing myself, as best as I can, to receive the blessing of God, trying not to be a barrier to that gift. This is the direct transmission of love from one soul to another. Later, and on reflection, I am sadly conscious of how difficult this was for me and how clumsy I am in spirit.

Assigned to Sister Maureen as my guide, there have been many other good moments after this. Further visits to Pound Lane, taking part in a number of discussions or dialogues as the BK sometimes call them. There have been visits to the BK's retreat house in Oxfordshire, with early morning meditation, teaching and excellent vegetarian food, which seems to involve mini-bus loads of Gujarati mothers and grandmothers, visiting the house and making delicious sweet biscuits and savouries. And, of course, there have been further teachings from Dadi Janki herself. All of this has been supplemented by some excellent books, tapes and CDs of teachings and meditations, including those of Sister Jayanti, the

European Director of the BK. I would not say that I have become a member of the family but I certainly feel that I am a second cousin and a welcome and regular guest. As a Quaker, I am very happy to be so.

The Brahma Kumaris was founded in the 1930s by a remarkable man, now referred to as Brahma Baba. In Hindu philosophy, Brahma means the creator but for the BK, and in this context, it means an instrument for renewal and Baba means Father. Brahma Kumaris means daughters of Brahma. Brahma Baba had been a successful diamond merchant in Calcutta but in the last part of his life he received and then passed on to his students a series of revelations about the nature of the world and our place in it and about our relationship both to God and to each other. A great many of his students were young women and, indeed, the organization has always been run by women. Some, like Dadi Janki, were there at its beginning and have dedicated the whole of their lives to its work.

The basic teaching of the Brahma Kumaris is Raja or Sovereign Yoga, the highest form of yoga that is expressed both in meditation and in a way of life in which the self is surrendered to God. The teaching is at one and the same time simple, direct and profound. Like Quakerism, it is based upon a doctrine and practice of love, with a belief in the intrinsic spirituality and goodness of each one of us. Indeed, again perhaps like us Quakers, the BK recognize that the global change that they work for can only arise from the changes that each one of us makes in our own lives.

However, there are aspects of the teaching that are especially of a BK flavour. For example, although we may see and, indeed, experience, ourselves in bodily form, each one of us is, in essence, said to be soul – not to have a soul but to be soul: I am soul, is a much-used mantra in BK meditations. Visualised as a point of light held in the forehead, in the position of the third eye, we can bring our soul being to rest in the light that is God. This light can be regarded as a point of light that is both eternal and without dimension. It is both a point and an ocean of light.

By the regular practice of surrendering ourselves to this light, mirroring the Christian notion of *Thy will be done*, the BK teach that we both open ourselves to divine service and find the guidance and confidence to be 'a good servant'. Dadi Janki is crystal clear on these matters and will often say something like: Well, what is the difficulty? It's clear isn't it? Just do it. I am struck by certain similarities with the teachings of George Fox: turning to the Light, dwelling in the Light. But in the teaching of the Brahma Kumaris there is no judgement, just a way of being.

Another particular characteristic that might seem difficult to Quakers is the notion of a cycle of history that starts with a Golden Age and then moves through a Silver and a Copper Age before coming to the darkest of all times, the Iron Age, the time in which we now live, the Kali Yuga. The Golden and Silver ages were a time of perfection, a time of paradise not dissimilar to the notion of the Garden of Eden before the Fall, although, as time passed, purity and power of spirit began to decline. To begin with this decline was only very slight but, as we entered the Copper Age, there was a further and more marked decline. As a consequence, happiness was lost and a spiritual search began. Thus it was that teachers such as Abraham, Buddha, Christ and Mohammad appeared. As each age has passed we have moved further and further from God. Indeed, we now reside at the lowest and darkest point of the cycle, the time of the Iron Age in which, with the growth of materialism, there is greater suffering, and loss of holiness. Nevertheless, it is thought that this time, barbaric and violent as it is, is the eventide before a new Golden Age. Indeed, this is called the Confluence Age – and it is thought, therefore, that this is a particularly important time to be making preparation by developing greater spirituality and nearness to God. Is this urgent turning to God what is meant in the Orthodox Christian notion of metanoia? There are certainly parallels in this and other traditions of oncoming catastrophe and turmoil followed by a new dawn, although this is not much discussed, I think, in Quaker circles.

I have to say that I do not find myself drawn to these matters and am rather influenced by the Buddha's advice that such speculation is unlikely to lead to enlightenment. In any event, and despite the evident degradation and disorder of the present time, I wonder whether such cycles are less a description of history and more a description of the moment-to-moment fluctuations of the spirit, the rise and fall of the experience of the divine each day and throughout our lives.

Perhaps for me, as a Quaker, the principal lesson of the Brahma Kumaris is their faith and their directness and commitment to a spiritual life, a lived experience that comes from a disciplined and constant practice that draws them towards God and sustains them in the presence of God. In this there is the enquiry of the mind but there is, most especially, a wisdom of the heart, something that arises from an inner intelligence of feeling and inspiration. When you are in its presence it is powerful and compelling.

By way of greeting and departure, the Brahma Kumaris say, Om Shanti, which means, I am a peaceful soul. It is a reminder of a way of being.

*Om Shanti.*

## The Author

David Cadman describes himself as a birthright Quaker who loves the teachings of the Buddha. Brought up in a Quaker family and at a Quaker school, he is now a husband, father and grandfather and works within the field of corporate responsibility, socially responsible investment and sustainability. He is a trustee of a number of charitable organisations including the Temenos Academy and the Prince of Wales's School of Traditional Arts. He represents the Prince of Wales on the Executive Committee of the Friends of Mount Athos and has visited Mount Athos each year for the last six years. His writings can be found at www.davidcadman.net.

# Searching for the Kingdom: a Tapestry

## Mary Cook

IT SEEMS THERE has been an order to my life, an order over which I have had no control. And in spite of outward appearances to the contrary, all has been well. The searching is the essence, the journeying, and without doubt, it has been a journey with Guidance. That is the joy.

### Sparkings – and some horses

My conscious searching began when I was nine. I was taken to a point-to-point race meeting – the first and only time I have been to a horse race – by a colleague of my father's I had not seen before. Before each race, the horses paraded, and it was from the start obvious which horse would win. I couldn't understand why everybody else couldn't see this. Point-to-points are for amateurs, and many farmers enter their own horses. But some professional stables would run novice horses as part of their training, and to me these horses stood out. It turned out that those in our party gained considerably when they realised what I was giving them!

From that time, not daring to think I could be more perceptive than my elders, I began to wonder if the future could be known. I realised that it was the truth behind prophesy I was seeking, that this was a gift of the spirit, and that the *search for the kingdom* was what I had embarked upon. I began to search the scriptures, to try to find adults who knew. I drew a blank at the Sunday schools I tried – they were little more than child-minders. I eventually decided to attend the Church of England to try to go deeper. During my early teens, our family was living in a semi-detached house, the attached semi was a Methodist manse. On our other side was a convent containing six Catholic nuns! I was friendly with both our neighbours, trying all the time to understand the differences and contradictions I was coming across.

As an only child, I spent much time alone, working things out – trying to understand what I found to be impenetrable truths.

Each bedtime, I would read the Bible – all through – searching for the depth that I needed.

*Seek ye first the Kingdom of Heaven.* This was the kernel. This was the commandment. More Bible searching wouldn't help – the Kingdom of Heaven is within you, around you. But how to find out more? Where? I asked and listened, but no-one seemed to know. *And nobody wanted to know that I needed to know.*

I would spend much time in prayer. In the middle of one night, I was awoken by a very bright light. It was outside and I had to go downstairs to see what it was. A bay window belonging to the convent looked directly into the room under my bedroom. Framed by this window, as in a triptych, were three figures, each one made up of a myriad of rays of golden light. The central figure held a sword, the point of which reached to the floor, like a sentry blocking the way. They had to be angels, but without wings. This vision convinced me that a Spiritual World existed. Where should I go from here? I felt I had had a glimpse – a disturbing glimpse. I resolved to look from as many different angles as I could find. When the time was right, I hoped I would be shown what to do.

### A touch of Zen – and my aunt

I visited my aunt in the depths of the countryside each weekend, and one day I noticed a book on her shelves I hadn't seen before. She had in fact picked it up in a local jumble sale!

It was hand printed on rice paper, hand sewn with ribbons, and instead of a cover, it had a sort of open box around it faced in silk, and fixed with an ivory toggle. Much of it was in Japanese. It was describing the life, art and poetry of a Zen monk, Ryokwan. I fell in love with his love of nature, and wondered how his religious way could be so bound up with a love of nature and simplicity. I loved nature, too, and felt a close affinity. I still read and cherish this book. Much later, I found out how Zen it had been.

## Hindu hints – and a friend

In the summer between A levels and college, I went with a friend on a fruit-picking holiday. We met two Indian boys, and I found that one of them was very interesting to listen to. I felt he knew more about what I was seeking than anyone I had yet met. He, too, was studying in London, so when I began my college course, we got in touch. He was a Brahmin. He had spent a year as a child in a monastery, and at home, since the age of five, some of each morning had been set aside for practising yoga under his mother's guidance. He had a serenity and self-control that had come from his upbringing.

Through him, I read some Upanishads, and found amazing parallels between what I was reading and what I had read in Christian literature. I also read the Bhagavad Gita in the translation by Swami Prabhavananda and Christopher Isherwood in which I found a description of Raja Yoga in a footnote. This description of an eight-fold path has probably influenced my spiritual life more than most teachings. It gave spiritual development a structure, only hints of which have I found elsewhere. I was very surprised when my friend came to church with me, and took communion. He, too, looked surprised – at my reaction. Didn't I know that it was possible to be a Hindu *and at the same time be a Christian?*

Later, I was very influenced by a book on the life of Ramakrishna, the Bengali saint who through intense effort lived in turn the Way of the Hindu, the Muslim, the Christian, the Buddhist, and attained the same spiritual goal and realisation through each path. The difference in the paths did not matter – the spiritual search itself was the universal truth.

Later on I joined a hatha yoga class and began to realise the self-control that comes from awareness of the body, the breath, and the mind. What I was finding in my own daily practices I did not find in the Church, and I had stopped attending regularly.

### Fragments – and a fellow student

While at music college I wrote a thesis on *World (Musical) Scale Systems*. I suppose I chose this thinking I might get insights into not only musical but also philosophical systems. One lunchtime in the college canteen, while talking about the thesis, someone mentioned a book that put all life and philosophy into a scale-like structure. It was Ouspensky's *In Search of the Miraculous*, which is as complete a record of the teachings of Gurdjieff as seems to exist. Gurdjieff preferred the sub-title, *Fragments of an Unknown Teaching*, thinking Ouspensky's title too sensational and too eye-catching. He preferred his teaching to be just for the few searchers who had been led to its discovery, and he made his own writings deliberately obscure until well into the book when, as if by magic, everything freed up.

Gurdjieff was an Armenian Jew who lived in Leningrad before the Revolution. A group of students and fellow seekers gathered around him, working intensely within a system of self-discovery that he was evolving. About the time of the Revolution he moved with some of his group to Fontainbleau, near Paris, where he continued this work, based on philosophical and practical discoveries made while searching in the Middle East, probably among Sufi masters. Whereas the structured philosophy he propounded appealed to me, his ideas regarding putting these into practice didn't. Some of his deep insights, though, have become an integral part of my thinking through my life. Even retrospectively, they have helped me crystallise something of what I have gleaned from different sources. For some years I meditated with a small group of friends the leader of which was also influenced by Gurdjieff.

## Yoga – and a guide

In my late twenties, I began to attend a yoga class taught by a quite different type of yoga teacher. Yoga was his life, and had been for a very long time. He was strong on *pranayama* (breath control), and he made sure we knew the reasons behind each *asana* (posture) we undertook. I approached his classes with body, mind and soul. Some of the meditation sessions were life-changing. When certain physical changes happened to me in my deep meditation, our teacher invited me to his home, where I was given certain books to read. One of them was *The 1000 Songs of Milarepa*. I realised that what we had been practising under our teacher's guidance was that which was being described by Milarepa – the Tibetan Buddhist master. The subtle quaking that happened to me, with nothing accompanying it except a peaceful acceptance, made me wonder if this had happened to the early Quakers under the guidance of George Fox, giving them their nickname. And it made me wonder if I shouldn't think about finding a Quaker meeting. I did, but thirty years on!

What the Bhagavad Gita, Milarepa and Gurdjieff were telling me was that much work must be done on the self – the physical, emotional, intellectual self/selves – before the spiritual self can be realised. Putting this next to Christianity where we are told that all we have to do is believe, at first it seemed contradictory. It is here that one needs to consider the variety of yogas (yokes, ways). Hatha yoga, the physical way has been followed to extreme by fakirs and the like, but otherwise is seen as the third step of Raja yoga. Bhakti yoga, the way of devotion, is the way practised by the monks, nuns, Christians who love their Lord with all their hearts, souls, minds and strengths. For these, to believe is enough! Many Hindus similarly revere their divinity, which may even be

Christ. Gana (Jnana) yoga is the intellectual path, which is described as limiting! Karma yoga is said to be the most practical, being the path of duty – duty to yourself, to your parents, to your family and to God. Your path is before you – follow it and your life will be blessed. *Seek ye first the Kingdom of Heaven, and all these things shall be added unto you.* This yoga and perhaps Jnana yoga remind me most of contemporary Quakerism.

Raja Yoga's eight steps are:
- Practice of moral virtues
- Regular habits of purity, contentment, study, austerity, and self-surrender to God
- Posture (Hatha yoga)
- Control of the vital energy with breathing exercises (pranayama)
- Withdrawal of the mind from sense objects
- Concentration
- Meditation
- Absorption in the consciousness of God

From a Quaker perspective, all of this seems far too self-centred, and I cannot see many Quakers thinking that anything above and beyond the first two steps would ever be necessary. They might well be right.

It is not the case, however, that Jesus simply asked his disciples to believe. He also instructed them to work on themselves as he had on himself during his forty day fast in the desert following his baptism. When his disciples had tried to heal certain complaints Jesus had said that the strength they needed for such work came only from prayer and fasting.

All these philosophies come from the same source; all lead in the same direction. None contradict. All have beauty within them.

### Indian Music – and a Muslim

Whilst I was practising yoga, I took a course of research into North Indian classical music. I mentioned to a friend that I proposed to study Indian music, and she happened to know of a sitar belonging to a friend of hers who had become a nun, who it turned out was willing for me to use it. It had no bridge or strings and some tuning pegs were missing. I was very fortunate to be tutored by a wonderful Muslim, a first class musician. He found me a bridge, and strings; the woodwork teacher of the school where I was teaching did a lathe demonstration with a class of boys, the outcome of which was that I completed my set of pegs! Playing the sitar meant I couldn't continue to play my violin which was my first instrument. The first finger of the left hand is in permanent contact with the string, which cuts it and hardens it in a way that it cannot be used on the violin. I never came to terms with the heavy amount of practice I required to play the sitar properly. Nor had I the cultural background which was absolutely necessary. I did not find this an easy choice.

North Indian classical music has a tradition that has been passed down in mainly Muslim families. Strange as this may seem with the current obsession with Muslim fundamentalism that restricts music and artistic freedom, the more I perceive its different facets. The study of an Indian musical instrument is in itself a spiritual way, though I was never told this. One has to realise things for oneself in this tradition. What we are told in life is never our own knowledge. What we find out for ourselves is ours for ever.

Though linked with Islam, this music, and especially sitar playing, is an integral yoga. People who have studied yoga will be aware of the concept of *chakras*, of energy channels, and of the importance of the spine as a type of electric cable through the body, connecting and enlivening each part. The yogic word for the spine is *dandi*. The same word is used for the neck of the sitar. The way that the music is woven through a *raga* (a scale pattern which is used to develop a very complex improvised composition) mirrors the opening of spiritual centres within the body. I haven't heard anyone voice this view. It is simply my observation.

## Islam – and a touch of Sufism

One afternoon, following a sitar lesson, my tutor was seeing me to the door. I don't recall how the conversation began, but Islam was mentioned. We had never talked about any religious topic, and this particular time was not a good one for discourse. I remember him saying something about my perhaps getting to know something about Islam. I remember feeling myself put in a difficult spot, and replied: I follow the teachings of Jesus, to which he replied: So do we. That was the first time I had realised how strong the connection is between Islam and Jesus, and I made up my mind to find a Koran.

I heard that Muslims didn't approve of translations of the Koran, and that reading the text in Arabic was recommended to all! Eventually, I obtained a translation of it, and was really taken by the passage around the birth of Jesus, *The House of Imran*. I recently went to a recording of BBC Wales' religious programme *All Things Considered*. One of the panel of four who was a Muslim made the comment that Islam without Jesus would be nothing.

I have recently attended some evenings of story telling in the style of the Sufis. Each story carried a pearl of wisdom. My eyes were opened to the deep truth in some of the *One Thousand and One Nights* stories that I'd known since childhood. I began to read the books of Idries Shah, and to learn about the Way of the Sufi. Sufism in its essence may be much more ancient than Islam, but nowadays, it has been absorbed within Islam and Sufis are described frequently as its mystics.

## Quakerism – and my mother

I have just recently realised the significance of some what I heard from my Brahmin friend. Religious insights are never lost, although as we grow older we generally feel there is more forgotten than retained. In my early teens I came across Quakerism, and remember a conversation I had with my mother. She said that Quakers were people she respected highly and that they were above us in every way. I asked what they believed in, and I felt then that I was at one with all I was told, more so than with any other religious group. I felt even then that one day I would join them. My parents were not religious although my mother became confirmed in the Church of England a year after I did. Her parents used to hold simple services in their own home during her early years. Her father would play the organ while anyone from the street was welcome to sing and pray with them. If I had to give my mother's family a label, I would call them lovers of their fellow men. I was brought up to find things out for myself. I think I was too intense about this task for my parents' liking, but I thank them to this day for their approach – one that I now realise to be rare in this world where a village, a town, or even a country is frequently defined by the religion of its inhabitants.

I had to wait till the time was right before the Quaker Way opened to me. It did some forty years later. I had trodden my own spiritual path, drawing threads from faith traditions and philosophical systems, yet feeling myself to be a student of Jesus all the while; feeling myself to be guided, immersed in the Spiritual, but not in a religion as such. I needed to become a Quaker for a different kind of spiritual development, a more social kind.

Deep down I may have learnt more from Jesus' teaching than from all that followed, or from the yogic philosophies, or Gurdjieff's – yet what I'd really been doing all along is looking for the essence of Jesus' teachings on the Kingdom of Heaven hidden within all other faiths and practices. Quakerism is the only Church I feel I can bring all my Eastern training to without feeling out of place. It is another thread in the weave, the blend, the Eternal Tapestry.

**The Author**

Mary Cook trained at the Guildhall School of Music and Drama, and as a teacher at London University. She taught music in Hemel Hempstead before moving to Gwent, South Wales, with her husband and daughter in 1982, where she became a peripatetic strings teacher. She found Quakers in the mid-nineties, and was accepted into membership a year later; she is currently convenor of the eldership and oversight committee in South Wales Monthly Meeting. She is still researching into the history and philosophy of beliefs, and finds much enjoyment playing chamber music with friends.

highly and that they were above us in every way. I asked what they believed in, and I felt then that I was at one with all I was told, more so than with any other religious group. I felt even then that one day I would join them. My parents were not religious although my mother became confirmed in the Church of England a year after I did. Her parents used to hold simple services in their own home during her early years. Her father would play the organ while anyone from the street was welcome to sing and pray with them. If I had to give my mother's family a label, I would call them lovers of their fellow men. I was brought up to find things out for myself. I think I was too intense about this task for my parents' liking, but I thank them to this day for their approach – one that I now realise to be rare in this world where a village, a town, or even a country is frequently defined by the religion of its inhabitants.

I had to wait till the time was right before the Quaker Way opened to me. It did some forty years later. I had trodden my own spiritual path, drawing threads from faith traditions and philosophical systems, yet feeling myself to be a student of Jesus all the while; feeling myself to be guided, immersed in the Spiritual, but not in a religion as such. I needed to become a Quaker for a different kind of spiritual development, a more social kind.

Deep down I may have learnt more from Jesus' teaching than from all that followed, or from the yogic philosophies, or Gurdjieff's – yet what I'd really been doing all along is looking for the essence of Jesus' teachings on the Kingdom of Heaven hidden within all other faiths and practices. Quakerism is the only Church I feel I can bring all my Eastern training to without feeling out of place. It is another thread in the weave, the blend, the Eternal Tapestry.

# The Author

Mary Cook trained at the Guildhall School of Music and Drama, and as a teacher at London University. She taught music in Hemel Hempstead before moving to Gwent, South Wales, with her husband and daughter in 1982, where she became a peripatetic strings teacher. She found Quakers in the mid-nineties, and was accepted into membership a year later; she is currently convenor of the eldership and oversight committee in South Wales Monthly Meeting. She is still researching into the history and philosophy of beliefs, and finds much enjoyment playing chamber music with friends.

# A Goddess-Loving Quaker Ponders Her Dilemmas

## Alison Leonard

AT A RECENT QUAKER retreat, I and about thirty other Quakers were asked to stand in the petals of a flower marked out on the floor of a large room. Each of the petals represented the sources of extra spiritual nourishment that we as individuals regularly draw on: the Christian tradition, Buddhist meditation, Eastern mysticism, the natural world, healing ministries such as Reiki, and so on, with the Quaker worshipping community as the flower's centre. Each person chose their appropriate petal. Some put their left foot in one petal and their right foot in another, and there were even acrobatics as Quakers put hands and feet in three or four different places.

This exercise acknowledged, in a visual and physical way, that our Quaker lives are fed by spiritual wisdom from outside the Quaker world. During the first three hundred years of Quakerism, this enrichment came from the Judaeo-Christian Bible and the accumulated wisdom of the Christian faith. During the last fifty years, historical and cultural changes have meant that we can draw on many other sources. The petals of our flower recognised this change and gave it a positive context of interest and sharing rather than a negative one of theological dispute.

My feet stood firmly in the petal marked Natural World. For the last seven or eight years I've been moving towards revering the earth's natural processes, honouring the feminine face of the divine, joining in pagan spiritual circles, and discovering the world of the goddess.

I was brought up firmly in the Christian tradition: Church of England at home, Methodist for nine years at a girls' boarding school. So I attended the colourful ritualistic Anglican services at the parish church during my time at home, while at school there were daily assemblies with lusty hymn-singing and a strong Biblical basis for weekly sermons and Scripture lessons. For some of my fellow pupils this was fine, because the Judaeo-Christian tradition fed them spiritually. For me, it was like being a vegetarian and having a feast of meat put in front of me. I was told There's food, and it *was* food. But it wasn't the right food for me. I didn't know why it wasn't right, and I kept on trying to make it right.

Looking back, it's clear that my problem was not with Jesus, who I still find an inspiration, but with the structure of the Church itself. It demanded obeisance to the invisible God, which generally translated into obedience to the all-too-visible male clergy. For a girl becoming a woman there were few possible roles beyond silent service. To use the term which emerged in the 1960s, the problem was patriarchy. That concept came a decade too late for me. As I grew from a shy child to a gawky teenager, I thought it was me who was wrong.

I was especially wrong when it came to the sacrament of Holy Communion. Week by week when I was among Anglicans, termly when I was a Methodist, I went up to the Lord's Table hoping to receive the promised essence of the divine. Week by week I returned to my pew having received nothing at all.

When I went to university I did some religious exploring. First I joined a Christian fundamentalist group; that didn't last long because I was studying philosophy and psychology and I wasn't willing to rubbish those insights. Then I was attracted to the Bah'ais. I found them gentle, thoughtful people, with peaceful, simple, internationalist ways and (I later realised) a theology not unlike the Quakers. But the cultural gap was too wide for me to join them. I tried going nowhere religious, staying in bed on a Sunday morning like my friends who would murmur 'Does Sunday *have* a morning?', but I couldn't kick the religious habit. So I settled down to working in a city mission to the poor (it was the 1960s and we still talked like that) and decided that if the divine wasn't going to commune with me, I'd find my spiritual path through communion with human beings.

Then, when I was in my 20s, I came across the Quaker Meeting for Worship. I fell into its depths immediately. Relief swept through me. No theology, no sacraments, no words. Just an inward journey supported by an outward community, with accompanying social and political witness. Bliss. For me as a feminist there was a special delight in the Quaker testimony to equality, because I found that in the Quaker world women and men work together according to their gifts.

It's 38 years since I went to my first Quaker Meeting for Worship. For most of that time I've been part of a large and thriving Meeting. I've looked after its children (as well as my own) and helped to nurture its spiritual life as an elder. I've joined in national Quaker affairs, mainly on the literature and publications side. I've only occasionally acted as clerk, which is odd, because one of my particular passions is the Quaker business method; in fact one of the reasons I'm still a Quaker is that we take the spiritual nature of decision-making seriously. The Quaker business method involves the whole community both in day-to-day practicalities and in big spiritual and moral challenges, and it makes provision for change and growth. Of course it doesn't always work that way, because we're fallible human beings, and we Quakers fall into bad power struggles just as we fall into empty phases of worship. But the ideal is still there to return to.

So what happened to my search for union with the divine? Did I find it in the quiet of Quaker Meeting for Worship? I did. Into its depths I could bring my passion and my despair, my many seekings and my few findings. There they would join the seekings and findings of my co-worshippers, to mingle like ingredients in the divine cooking pot as, individually and together, we moved inward and emerged changed. In Thomas Kelly's words (*Quaker Faith & Practice* 2.38), we *found our separate lives were all one life, within whom we live and move and have our being.*

Yet, as I went about my daily life, I was still a rebel against institutional Christianity. I couldn't come across someone in a clerical dog-collar without arguing with him (or, after the long struggle by Anglican women, occasionally with her). I did wonder why. Maybe I was missing the intellectual discipline of theology? No, it wasn't that. It was that I was an imaginative person who loved symbols and metaphors, and I was missing an image of the divine.

It didn't seem a problem, as such. The Meeting for Worship was where I knew I belonged, and the quiet deep openness to the divine fed me with living food. But still there was a space.

That vacant space was given particular emphasis in the early 1980s when I joined the local Women for Peace group to campaign against Cruise nuclear missiles being sited in this country. In the summer of 1983 we set off on a two-week march from Chester to Greenham Common. To my amazement and shock, our dedicated group fell apart in a mess of accusation and counter-accusation.

Here I was, a feminist and a pacifist, among a group of women fighting. How could that be?

Clearly, feminism was not enough. Nor was principled pacifism. There had to be a spiritual basis for the necessary change from patriarchy to equality, from domination to respect. But how? Britain was not about to convert to Quakerism. In any case, consciously bringing about that sort of change didn't seem to me to be the core purpose of Quakerism. My vision of the Quaker way is not that it draws others into itself so as to save the world on its own, but that it welcomes those who discover it, nurtures their integrity, and supports their search for ways to act authentically in whatever context is right for them.

After the debacle of the Greenham march, life went on. I was asked to be part of the group to tackle the revision of the main Quaker book (which in 1995 became *Quaker Faith and Practice*) and joyfully accepted. I withdrew from anti-nuclear campaigning to put my pacifism into issues like ending corporal punishment in schools.

Then, in the summer of 1996, I was co-tutoring at Woodbrooke Quaker Study Centre in Birmingham on a course for people wanting to reflect on their spiritual journey in some depth. A young woman participant told me that her worship was directed towards the Goddess. One afternoon she and I sat on the bench on the far side of the lake that lies in Woodbrooke's lovely garden, and she offered to recite a Goddess prayer. I said I'd be glad of it, and as I listened, I was moved to my bones.

At that moment, I didn't fully realise the impact this would have on me: that it was, in fact, the start of a new life in which I could cut loose from patriarchy and soak myself in the womanly face of the divine. As the years progressed, I would attend the annual UK Goddess Conference, make pilgrimages to ancient sacred sites, create personal altars, take part in ceremonies led by priestesses, watch the movement of sun and moon and stars and seasons, and touch the earth in a thousand ways. Some of these spiritual practices flatly contradict the priestless, un-ceremonial, times-and-seasons-free ways of Quakers. Yet I have never felt more of a Quaker.

My first chance to touch the world of the Goddess was at the Goddess Conference, which had just got going as an annual summer event in Glastonbury, Somerset. I'd heard about the Conference from Rose Flint, a friend and colleague and a wonderful poet of earth-spirit. Early in the year 1997, before I went to my first Goddess Conference, Rose sent me a card for January 31st/ February 1st, saying 'Happy Imbolc'. Imbolc? What did the word mean? Other, equally mysterious, words – 'Beltane', 'Lughnasa', 'Samhain' – wandered across my consciousness. Gradually I began to learn about the Celtic wheel of the year, the marking of the seasons which was traditional in the pre-Christian culture of these islands and which the Church absorbed and adopted with their own names and rituals. At the Conference I learned about the ways in which these festivals have been celebrated in our north European corner of the world. There could be fires and candles, music and drumming and dancing, or quiet night watches under the stars. There would be reverence for the stirrings of new life at Imbolc, a celebration of the glory of spring and sexual fulfilment at Beltane (which remains with us as May Day), thanksgiving for the fullness of the grain at Lammas or Lughnasa, and a recognition of the closeness of the spirit world at Samhain. (Every year I'm distressed by the degradation of this deeply reverent celebration of past souls into the modern, tricksy-treaty, commercialised Hallowe'en.) I knew that early Quakers had rejected times and seasons on powerful theological grounds relevant to their time and mindset. But it seemed wonderful to me, three hundred and fifty years on and living in an urban, technological culture, to connect with the cycle of nature. It seems ever more wonderful the longer I do it.

At first it was strange to use the word pagan for these insights and practices. Paganism has had a bad press for thousands of years, ever since monotheism discovered how to write its own story. In Europe, as the early adherents of the Christian religion struggled to establish Christianity as the dominant faith, they vilified all things pagan. This vilification lurks even today, with the term still sounding like an insult in some contexts. The word pagan actually comes from the same source as peasant, meaning of the countryside; it means rural, homespun, ordinary-people-based, rather than head-of-state-based as the monotheistic religions have been. Time and again, because they're part of popular culture rather than part of the structure of dominance, pagan attitudes and imagery have almost been wiped out. Probably some aspects *have* been wiped out. But pagan ways have never wholly disappeared, and keep on re-appearing in the works of stonemasons and storytellers, artists and poets.

As I sporadically entered this world, an important lesson for me to learn was that the pagan Goddess doesn't in any way replace the God of monotheistic religions. There are many thousands of Goddess stories and images. Almost every language and culture has them. In each culture, myths of the Goddess have been passed down from generation to generation in oral form, rather than in writing, so that they change and develop rather than becoming frozen as scriptural texts. Each and every name of the Goddess is a symbol of some aspect of the eternal female principle. The Goddess is not a single Being, set apart from the natural world and the everyday life of the planet. Quite the reverse. All the stories and songs and images of goddesses are facets of the whole, signposts to the inward and outward creative impulse which turns the earth on its axis and sustains it, body and soul.

Another vital lesson was that the divine female must unite with the divine male – the Goddess with the God. That's the way growth comes. At Newgrange, a World Heritage site near Drogheda in Ireland, a huge earth mound protects a ceremonial stone passage shaped like the human birth canal, and that passage-way is penetrated by the sun for just seventeen minutes every year, at dawn on the Winter Solstice. During the ceremonies accompanying this and similar events at other ancient sites, our European ancestors celebrated the physical and metaphysical union of female with male which lies at the heart of all creation, and those celebrations are now being revived. And if it seems that, among those who are involved in this revival, the female side of the seesaw is pressing harder than the male, maybe that's a necessary redressing of the balance after millennia of patriarchy so that in due course full and equal union can be restored.

So which are the goddesses that most appeal to me and to people like me? In the current pagan revival, people tend to choose the images and stories most relevant in our generation and culture. One of my favourite stories is about the

Welsh goddess Ceridwen, who throws into her great cauldron all the rotten things she can find (*Eye of newt and toe of frog*, say the witches in *Macbeth*) until, after a year and a day's stirring, three drops of inspiration spit out. In my imagination, I can throw into Ceridwen's cauldron all the rotten experiences of my life, even my own misdeeds, so that she can stir and stir and eventually, if I'm patient, transform it all into distilled illumination. This seems far more positive and useful than the sin and self-abasement I was brought up with.

Another goddess I find attractive is Bridget, whose stories and altars originated in Ireland and who is still revered there as goddess and as Christian saint. I'm a writer, so I love her as goddess of poetry. But she also represents healing and smithcraft (a combination which seems marvellously to combine earthy work and airy spirituality) and she tenderly looks after the needs of young women. Two nuns came from Kildare to the Goddess Conference of 2004 and told us how strongly the feeling is growing in Ireland that the Christian Bridget and the pagan Bridget are united, indivisible, one.

None of these goddesses, Isis, Astarte, Inanna, Dana, Hera, Kali, Demeter, Parvati, Coatlicue, Oshun and the rest, or their male counterparts for that matter, are beings, solid, unalterable. Like the Greek and Roman goddesses and gods that my generation learnt about at school, they have attributes and stories attached to them, and represent aspects of the divine: often sustaining and creative, but sometimes also threatening and even destructive, because that's the way of the world we live in and we need to learn to live with all its aspects. The fundamental pagan principle is Life, followed by Death, followed by Regeneration, followed by Life again. Accepting this basic cyclical principle, realising that death is a physical necessity but feeds the life to come, helps me to come to terms with the prospect of my own physical body's decay and inevitable death.

At the Goddess Conferences I've bumped into quite a few other Quakers, both women and men. I sat with one of them on a cool stone step in Glastonbury High Street discussing the pros and cons of the priestesses who were part of this goddess scene. How can we put up with these women, we asked each other (forgetting for the moment that there are a few goddess-loving priests as well), when the whole of Quaker history is bound up with the rejection of hireling priests?

Gradually I began to see the answer to this. These pagan priestesses and priests are voluntary and unpaid. They aren't ordained in the way the Christian priests are, set apart from the rest, full-time representatives of the Divine. They're trained for a specific purpose: to conduct ceremonies. When a ceremony is required, they conduct it in a priestly way. Afterwards they go back into the crowd. This is a way of dealing with the knotty issue of power, just as Nominations procedures cope with issues of power in a Quaker context. Having said that, in my view the pagan world lacks the organisational genius of a George Fox and the Society of Friends' 350 years of experience in conflict management, and could learn a great deal from Quaker ways.

Ceremony and ritual are aspects of the pagan world that a Quaker can sit uneasily with. Though I was confused at first, it wasn't long before I was finding these ceremonies deeply moving. I discovered that, if they were well-conducted, they could move me into a different place of consciousness. The celebrations of the elements – Earth, Air, Fire and Water – as sacred presences of the Goddess in our midst resonated with me so powerfully that my intellect as well as my emotions started to acknowledge them as valid. Looking at the historical record, I see that such rituals have been part of spiritual practice since the beginning of human experience, and looking at it philosophically, I realise that honouring earthly elements as sacred means taking responsibility for the earth rather than trying to dominate it. My Quaker friend and I, sitting on that cool stone step, acknowledged that our Quaker practice also has elements of ritual about it – the timing, the circle, the placing of the elders and the clock, the creation of quiet expectancy – which are carefully nurtured by elders. The ceremonies at the Goddess Conference were different in manner, in colour and dancing and story, but they didn't feel alien to me as a Quaker. They felt creative and energising.

Early one morning, I climbed up Glastonbury Tor to take part in a dawn ritual. It was dull and cloudy. I danced in a circle with the others, wondering why I'd bothered to get up so early. And then, against all expectation, I experienced my first communion. It was wonderfully simple: two women took a wooden bowl of seeds and a clay goblet of drink and passed them round. As I nibbled the seeds and sipped the drink, all those years of waiting fell down the hill, and for me at that moment, as I put it in a poem later, 'There was nothing that was not me, / or Spirit, or wonder, or seed, or dancing'. Two priestesses had got up before dawn to prepare the elements of the ceremony, then they'd carried the elements up the hill and let the Spirit move as it willed. That Spirit had touched me, entered me, and made me feel whole.

As the years have gone on, I've increasingly come to know the Earth as my sacred Mother. I garden and cook, I notice the ways of animals and birds, I watch the stars in their courses, I feel the seasons as they turn. Of the myriad ways in which I love the Earth, the stone circles and passage graves created by long-ago peoples feel particularly special to me, and I spend holidays seeking out places like Callanish on the Isle of Lewis in Scotland or Gavrinis in Brittany. These journeys are like pilgrimages. When I come back, I put small items from those places – pebbles and shells and feathers and flotsam and fragments of twisted twig – on a mantelshelf or windowsill, carefully arranging them with a sense of sacredness, like an altar. After the visit to Callanish Stone Circle I wrote another poem, which ended: 'For this is where your mother / built her altar, and fashioned it / in awe to face the wind and sun and sea, / not to bow down, but to stand, / shoeless, with her own song.' *Not to bow down, but to stand.* This is the essence of Goddess ways to me. The patriarchal system asked me to bow down before a Lord and Master. The Goddess invites me to stand in a circle of my friends and forebears and fellow-creatures. To me, this sits beautifully in harmony with Quaker ways. It also shows me how much I've learned over the years from the writings of the Quaker Women's Group, who for 30 years or more have nurtured a specifically womanly spirituality among Quakers.

When I bring my Goddess consciousness to Meeting for Worship, my spiritual experiences take their place alongside the spiritual experiences of all other Quakers. Occasionally I minister from that place in my heart. But more often I simply chat about my Goddess exploration to Quakers during coffee after Meeting, just as when I'm in Goddess circles I chat to people there about being a Quaker.

People ask me whether there might ever come a point where I have to choose between the Quaker way and the Goddess way. My confident reply is that there's no need to choose. But that may be a little disingenuous. There are times when choices have to be made: where two events clash in time, for instance, as Britain Yearly Meeting or the Summer Gathering sometimes clash with the Goddess Conference. On these occasions I've tended to choose the Goddess Conference, because that's my only week of concentrated Goddess space in the year, whereas my Quaker life goes on all the 51 other weeks. This choice demonstrates the larger choice that I'm making all the time. I haven't sought out a local pagan group or goddess network. I don't want to. My spiritual community is my Quaker Meeting, the Meeting for Worship, the local and district business meetings. Week by week my diary contains entries like MM Elders, Children's Committee, a note to myself to prepare PM newsletter or to go to (a happy local invention) Quaker pub night. Interwoven with these are my readings of Goddess books, my porings over star-charts and the re-arrangings of my small altars according to the season or the items that I've brought back from my most recent pilgrimage. But my core schedule is around the

Quaker calendar. I regularly read from *The Once and Future Goddess* and *The Goddess Companion*, but my Bible is *Quaker Faith & Practice*.

Liz Perkins, a Quaker friend who is part of a little group who overlap the two spiritual paths, says: My Quaker experience made me very comfortable with speaking my own truths as part of home-grown ritual – and this made her so noticeable in the Goddess movement that she was challenged to train as a priestess. In doing so, she says: I learnt more about the many faces of the Goddess, was supported in developing my own spiritual practice, discovered my love of the natural world was a necessity not an optional extra, and learnt a lot of new skills for helping others – all of which could be fed back into her Quaker life when the time was right. Liz's husband Lucus Greenwood, who left Quakers and later trained as a priest in the Goddess tradition, writes: I cherish my dreams, I read Goddess literature, and I've studied with Kathy Jones, who founded the Goddess Conference. But recently I rediscovered my basically Quaker inner stance, and together with my wife I've found a Meeting where I feel welcomed as a lovingly sceptical attender.

Our little group of Quakers who also go to Goddess Conferences are starting to meet together twice a year at places like Woodbrooke or Charney Manor. We spend our time talking through the issues that I'm exploring here, but more importantly, we share our hopes and fears and insights at a deep level, using both Quaker worship and the imagery and spiritual practices of the Goddess world. We practice eldership and oversight in a conscious way, grounding our spiritual searches in a shared responsibility.

In true Quaker fashion, I and these others aren't trying to proselytise, to persuade the Society of Friends to go pagan. In fact, I see that the movement we're a part of is growing in British and European society as a whole. Everywhere you look, especially in the Green movement, patriarchal structures are giving way to (or more often, struggling alongside) earth-centred spiritual and political attitudes. Patriarchy is under tremendous strain, and it's clear that men as well as women have suffered from patriarchal expectations. During the decades of the feminist movement, women realised what they'd lost by assuming they should be dependent, pretty, always putting men's needs and values before their own. More recently it's become only too obvious that men and boys are greatly inhibited, not least in their educational attainment, by expectations that they should be tough, unfeeling, distant. The pagan principle that growth comes through the divine female uniting with the divine male, the Goddess with the God, has a lot to teach us as we struggle to rediscover our place in the divine scheme of things. We Quakers, with our practical vision of gender equality, our openness to new light, from whatever source it may come, and our eagerness to prevent the world from sliding into self-destruction, are ideally placed to appreciate and benefit from this principle.

I look back over the patriarchal project of the last few thousand years and see it as a well-meant mistake, one of a collection of philosophies and theologies that has taken us to the brink of extinction. Two decades ago it looked as though that extinction would come from nuclear war. Now the environmental crisis is drawing us towards a more long-drawn-out extinction. Man's domination of nature, fuelled (intentionally or unintentionally) by quotations from the Judaeo-Christian Bible about man being given by God dominion ... over every creeping thing that creepeth upon the earth, needs to give way to humility and gratitude to the rest of the created world. A spiritual philosophy that connects humankind with all other natural things is one which may – possibly, hopefully – turn us around from disaster.

Setting these wider philosophical speculations aside, I can see that I'm a woman of my time. I've been caught up with the spiritual explorations of the 1960s, with the peace campaigning of the 1980s, and with the Green movement of the present day. I don't any longer believe (if I ever believed) that there is One Truth. I think we each seek out, from among the many truths, the ones which speak to us and move us and serve us in our lives. For me, the quiet Quaker way and the busy Quaker community are my bread-and-butter, while Goddess stories and rituals and images are the jam. I've found real food at last, a veritable feast, which I can eat with joy and integrity and which looks set to nourish me all my days.

**The Author**

Alison Leonard has written fiction for children and young people, plays for BBC radio and two books on life as a spiritual journey. Now in semi-retirement, she continues to write for pleasure. She is married with two adult daughters, and apart from being a lady of letters (to MPs, local papers etc on political matters), her main preoccupations are Friends (Quakers) and friends (important people in life), some of whom overlap. Spending time with birds and plants provides her chief relaxation.

# Interfaith Influences on Spiritual Development

## Judy Moody-Stuart

THE KINGDOM OF God is the great space-time of spiritual experience where riches and mysteries lie for all seekers to find and to share.

In 1959 a visit to Meeting for Worship at Brighton Friends Meeting House and a copy of Christian Faith and Practice in the Experience of Friends, preceded by a three months geological expedition to Spitsbergen under the leadership of the principled Quaker Brian Harland, aroused my interest in Quakerism. Though I had abandoned my Anglican upbringing I was still assuming that there would be an option to enter the Kingdom of God should I ever encounter such an entity.

Then in 1968, in Borneo among upriver Ulu animists, I discovered the possibility of deep communication with few words. I was faced with issues completely new to me: the social rules of the longhouse; the attitude of the Islamic Brunei government to the Ulu peoples; the social significance of head hunting; the loss of life caused by outlawing. It occurred to me that a single human being could be living parallel lives: one in the technically developed coastal oil towns and the other up in the misty primary and secondary rain forests.

To be affected spiritually by another person one needs only to lower the protective barriers and sit open. People who are comfortable with themselves can readily do this. Picture me as a European high-nose-bridged-dutch-type-person orang belanda based in the coastal oil community for five and a half years . I learned Malay and went upriver fairly regularly as grants officer of the voluntary Community Service Council to assess claims for community cash assistance. Though my insights were partial and not necessarily valid I have been permanently affected by them.

I was once perched, pregnant and with our two elder boys, on the wooden rail of a Chinese-run trading post two days upriver past unnavigable rapids. With me, discussing in our joint second language Malay, were two tattooed Kayan women, also with small children. We talked about the worry of aging parents, how to keep your man happy, the children's health and food – universal subjects that testify to the equality and oneness of humankind. I investigated their tattooing, they investigated our curly red hair and freckles.

Among the Kelabit, one of the tests of being a good housewife was still to be able to make your husband a leaf-wrapped block of pure white boiled rice to take hunting, the purity being all important. To this end all germ and husk and anything else was swept traditionally into a great glazed jar to ferment into an aseptic and nutritious brew of beer. Alas, temperance rules originally developed in the nineteenth century industrial slums of Britain and suggested to the Kelabit by Christian missionaries deprived them of this drink and have led to a deterioration of their health. Alcohol nonetheless was acceptable to the men's cash-generating lives at the coast.

I saw Punans, pale skinned jungle nomads, struggling to settle by the rivers upland so that their children would be educated, though they, the parents, would be under government control. In spite of my encouragement, their spirits were too low to tell their cultural stories to others in order to write them down and preserve them. I sat in longhouses under dusty rattan nets holding human skull collections, drinking home-distilled alcohol from the rice brews, watched offerings poured to the spirits and chickens ritually killed. There were elaborately carved hanging dishes of aromatic food to allow the spirits of the dead to share the pleasures of the living. Men and women displayed their bodies in formal dances expressing communally accepted meanings. There was a reassuring simplicity in these traditional cultural settings that resonated with our Quaker testimony.

Upriver in Borneo social structures arise in response to what is a universal human problem: the dichotomy between *individuals with their wishes* as against *the expectations of their society*. The animist attitude gives a community the freedom to develop its own religious practice in a small-scale Congregationalist style, yet an individual must conform to community norms in order to survive.

It was when we moved from Borneo to Melbourne in Australia that I found a Quaker Meeting. Melbourne Quakers were in the forefront of urging respect for the Aborigines and their dreamtime stories. Over the four years my husband and I with our four children were in Australia, we were regular attenders at the Quaker Meeting. I did not feel the need to become a Member but consolidated the position of happy seeker.

Throughout our international life I have continued to respect and rely on the strong faith of others, slotting into a new community and always needing the companionship of those active in some spirit-led enterprise. While we were in Lagos I met some Nigerian Quakers and, rather self-consciously, began to call myself a Quaker.

Then, when the opportunity presented itself, I was ready for Islam. We had Muslim friends in Nigeria and drove across the Sahara with Ibrahim Ahmad, a Malaysian Muslim engineer. It was not until we started our four years in Turkey, which was followed by another four in West Malaysia that I felt the full interest and warmth of Islam.

Living in serial and often parallel social environments I became aware that there are many truths, that living truthfully might call for different and contradictory behaviour in different places.

In Istanbul we lived in a villa in a compound built by Sephardic Jews who had been driven from Spain by Ferdinand and Isabella and had lived freely since the 15th century as a thirty thousand strong community, still speaking Spanish at home.

The Muslim call to prayer soars five times every day in Istanbul and all kinds of spiritual and religious activities flourish. As a woman I was able to visit any of the many mosques even at prayer time and slip into the women's area at the back. One afternoon in the little Yahya Efendi mosque three old ladies tried to get me to become a Muslim : *You need only say 'There is no God but Allah and Mohammed is his prophet' three times and you can immediately belong,* they urged. Westerners imagine Muslim women to be suppressed, but that does not imply powerlessness: it is just that a different social geometry operates.

We witnessed a Sema of whirling dervishes. Each wears a hat like a tombstone (memento mori), keeps the heart in his axis of revolution – all in obedience to the sheikh. I tried it and can whirl myself with one arm held up to receive grace from God and the other outstretched to share it with man.

The Sufi tradition is of an individualistic Islam: paradoxical since the term Islam means submission to discipline. It is traditionally mistrusted by orthodox Muslims. There is something at the core of it that Quakers can recognise: the yearning for God, often expressed like the Jewish Song of Solomon as a man for his Lover. The integrity of creation is palpable in Sema. Mevlana-Celaluddin Rumi, the founder of the mystical Mevlevi sect of Dervishes (travelling monks) readily expressed it. The Turkish poet Yunus Emre wrote of the sound of the reed flute (ney) as it yearns for its old place by the lake from which it was taken, the wind whistling softly over the reed beds.. It is wonderful to experience in another culture's mystical tradition the realisation of one's own insights.

When we moved to Kuala Lumpur I made a study of Islamic banking and economics and learnt something of the reasons that the Prophet forbade usury. In Islam commerce is based on trust, money represents goods and services, and risk is shared between financiers and merchants alike. In this way, Islam compares readily with Quaker testimonies. It is enlightening to see how, in both systems, the human need for certitude in righteousness can override fundamental openness and equality.

In Malaysia there is a small organisation Sisters in Islam, started in the 1980s with a few professional Malay women who had professional standing in Kuala Lumpur society. Amongst them was a linguist who could advise them on fresh interpretations in the Arabic of Shari'ah law. They met regularly to study. They found that some family law relating especially to women was in contradiction to current, official, male, religious interpretations. Through peaceful, quiet, articulate conviction they have challenged and changed public judgements.

What I have gained from living among other faiths is the realisation that adherence to principles is a privilege, even a luxury, but that to be sure that one is right is a step too far. I found confirmation that if a single prime mover is worshipped without fear then the revelations of this God refer to and are identical with that God that is. Religion can be a rich man-made cultural art form. Seeking and recognising the essential sameness of the yearning, however patterned it is by the variety of historical, cultural, genetic and geographical backgrounds, infallibly brings people together. Humble seekers reach one another in the things that are eternal.

## The Author

Judy Moody-Stuart of Chichester Monthly Meeting grew up in Sussex, graduated in Natural Science as a Chemist, and then spent 5 years researching 100 million year old Wealdon fern spore species at Cambridge University. Currently supports small scale social projects in the UK and abroad, she is a Trustee of Quaker Social Action, and is interested in education, violence reduction and informal community archiving. She speaks Dutch, French, Malay and Turkish having accompanied her geologist husband for 35 years to work in several primarily Muslim countries.

# "Some of my best Friends......."

## John Dunston

IT SEEMED, AS THE saying goes, a good idea at the time.

Here was an advertisement from a Quaker school, intending to appoint a new Head: a Quaker or at the very least, someone in sympathy with the values and aims of Quakers.

What exactly were those values and aims? Could a non-Friend be in sympathy with them without embracing Quakerism? Did the Governors really think it would be possible to appoint someone who was not a Quaker as the Head of a Quaker school? There was only one way to find out.

And so, with one very personal letter of application, events began to take their course, a course that would lead my career, and my life and future family, in a direction wholly unexpected. For I was born and brought up within the Jewish faith. Although, like so many, I had heard of the Quakers (generally good things, of course, decent, prison-reforming, and so on), I had never envisaged for a moment that the next fifteen years would be spent so closely involved with the Society of Friends and its schools.

Connections, though, have always intrigued me. My parents had both come to this country in the late 1930's, refugees from Nazi-occupied Austria. My father had lost many of his family, including his own parents and sister, in the Holocaust; my mother's parents had been more fortunate, one of them surviving Dachau and Buchenwald, before they were, miraculously, able to come to England through the intervention of a Quaker couple in Leeds. These kind and selfless people had acted as guarantors for them, finding accommodation to help them rebuild their lives here. Without that couple, they might never have made it out of Hitler's Europe.

We all have stories of our families with which we grow through childhood and which become part of us. That was one of mine. It remained a story until I myself came upon Quakers and began my own encounter with them.

The moment on a stormy winter's evening in 1989 when I was offered the post of Head of Sibford School was the moment when that encounter really began. The unbearable tension of a series of interviews was spread over several weeks. On the final day, I was called back after the Governors' meeting for worship for one final interview, to explore with them that most critical aspect: how could they be convinced that they were being led to appoint a Jew as the Head of this Quaker school?

What my wife and I discovered the instant I accepted the post was a two way bond of love between the members of the School Committee and their new Head as they recognised how much more united they were than anything that could possibly have kept them apart. How strong were the spiritual ties that would surely see them through the inevitable challenges that lay ahead.

What we seemed to have uncovered were two of the great truths common to both Quakerism and Judaism: that neither faith had a monopoly of truth; that, notwithstanding the appalling history of ignorance, prejudice and persecution to which both religions had been subjected, they were now able to co-operate in the education of the young.

I began to learn about silence in worship, in business, and in school. Since, in my experience, Jews have never been terribly good at silence, there was much to learn. Sibford School was – it always had been and I know remains today – a place where the individual matters, a place to strengthen faith in oneself and in those around, a place of hope and affirmation, of restorative power, a place where miracles are achieved.

During my six and a half years as Head there, those values and aims began to take on substance, as all of us in the school community tried daily to reflect them in our dealings with each other, and in our vision for the future. I was upheld greatly by the wisdom and love of weighty Quakers on and outside the School Committee, in and outside the local Meeting. I learned also of Quakers' ambivalence towards Quaker schools, indeed towards independent schools in general, though any negative feelings about Sibford were somewhat tempered by recognising the often difficult backgrounds that pupils had had to survive before they came to the school. So many of them had learning difficulties and had been rejected by other schools. In other words, if there had to be fee-paying Quaker schools, a Sibford might just about be acceptable. It was also a school that had never been abundantly endowed with reserves or resources which seemed to go down well with Quakers.

At the other end of the Quaker schools spectrum stood Leighton Park – outwardly opulent, graciously endowed with splendid buildings – and not, therefore, held in such warm affection by members of the Society except, of course, by those who really knew it. While at Sibford, I had gained hugely from the fellowship of the heads and deputies of the other Quaker schools. There are strong links between all the schools, a similar ethos, similar values, and the same response to that of God in everyone, ran through them all. It was the revelation of what an education within Quaker principles could mean, even in a school with very few Quaker pupils, that led me to feel that this is where my future ought to lie, if at all possible. With greater knowledge this time, and consequently with greater trepidation, I applied for the headship of Leighton Park when it came up.

There were even more interviews than for Sibford: seven including one with a panel of pupils. Once again, having reached the final stages, religion was, rightly, a key issue. What about the testimonies? asked one Governor, a massive question that seemed suddenly to land from nowhere. More pragmatically one of the pupil interviewers had asked earlier, how would you make us work harder?. Later I understood why. I must have got something right for I learned later during that final interminable evening that I was to be offered the post. It was, by chance, April Fools' Day, the very date on which, six years earlier, my contract at Sibford had begun.

My wife and I had been married less than two years when we moved to Sibford; our two children have spent all their secondary education so far at Leighton Park. For this Jewish family the encounter with Quakerism has been a formative influence. Our Judaism has been a bedrock of our family life in both good times and bad. How fortunate, how rare, to have been able to live this part of our lives within not one but two Quaker communities.

Over the past fifteen years, I have been struck so often by points of profound contact between the two faiths. In his essay *Coming Home*, Gerald Priestland wrote: since Quakers have no test of faith, or Creed, each of us can only speak for himself. Now, Judaism does of course have a body of belief, which can be summed up in its great proclamation that there is only one God in whose image all humans are made. This leads directly to the commandment in the Book of Leviticus (19.18) to love one's neighbour as oneself. That, as the teacher Hillel pointed out, is the whole of Jewish law; all the rest is commentary.

But, and it is an important *but*, so many of the prayers in the Jewish liturgy begin *Our God and God of our fathers*. It is not enough to inherit the faith that has been handed down from previous generations, strong though that may be, for it may be learned without thought or reasoning. Everyone, in every generation, must attempt to reach faith through his own searching and thinking, to make it their own through personal experience. Or, as George Fox might have expressed it, *And this I knew experimentally.*

This direct relationship between each of us as individuals and God, with no need for the intercession of priests, is a reflection of the common understanding shared by both Judaism and Quakerism: that there can be a real dialogue in which both man and God, we trust, listen to each other.

Strange as that may sound when talking about religion and the spirit, the two faiths are intensely earthbound. For Jews, whatever might lie in store in the next world – whatever, indeed, that may be – is of less importance than the way our lives are led while we are here. Jews recognise that to love God truly one must first love man. In the words of Moses Mendelssohn, *to leave the world a little better for our sojourn in it.* Konrad Braun wrote: *Enormous is the amount of wrong in the world...Love, mercy and pity command us to do our best to right these wrongs, to oppose iniquity and to see more justice done to those who suffer from injustice.*

Both Judaism and Quakerism have been major forces of social good over the centuries. Though the language in which they express it may be different, both Jews and Quakers hold the creation of community dear, emphasising service and loving deeds.

Yes, and what about the testimonies? Although Quakers claim, with some justification, not to have a creed that is the test of membership, the principles, called the Testimonies, of Truth, Equality, Simplicity and Peace, are nonetheless a considerable binding force within the Religious Society of Friends. Indeed, in an age in which faith itself is under threat, at least in the West, as never before, it would be difficult to sustain a religious body that was not underpinned by common beliefs and values. In this context, I have often thought back to the wording of that Sibford advert.

The four Testimonies themselves reflect an understanding of man and his place in the world, in which the role of God is both paramount and unfathomable. The Testimonies are exhortations to a way of life which ought to make the world a better place. Our efforts, though, however genuine and energetic they might be, are incomplete without faith. Mary F Smith, writing in 1936, realised her own *inability to do even a familiar job, as it truly should be done, unless (she was) in touch with eternity, unless (she do) it unto God.*

For Jews, at least three of those testimonies have been at the heart of their experience. God is seen as the God of Truth, to whom they have turned, on whom they have relied even when reason suggested they should do otherwise: for example, during the Crusades, the Inquisition or the Holocaust. The Psalms remind us that we praise God for truth: the truth of God and his love for all mankind is a reality for Jews, as is the equality of all people as part of God's creation. The vision of a time when that ideal will be realised in the world is a powerful incentive to work towards it. Since the earliest days, peace has been the eternal hope of the Jews. In one sense, the Sabbath represents a glimpse each week of that peace. During these awful years of conflict in the Middle East, it is hard, to remember that throughout the millennia, Jews have prayed and acted constantly for peace. One of the most frequently recited prayers in the Jewish liturgy reflects just that: *May He who makes peace in the highest bring this peace upon us, upon all Israel, and upon the world.*

Simplicity? This is trickier, since of course Jewish observance in the home and in everyday life is rarely simple. However, the point of all the customs and traditions is, in the end, to reinforce the most basic and uncomplicated fact of Jewish life: that all life is sacred, that there is no distinction between the sacred and the secular, and that the multitude of blessings over the simplest acts, the apparently complicated rules of diet and observance, are but a reminder of those simple truths. *Quaker Faith and Practice* quotes North Carolina Yearly Meeting: *Inwardly, simplicity is spiritual detachment from the things of this world as part of the effort to fulfil the first commandment: to love God with all of the heart and mind and strength* – words which themselves are taken from the Shema, the most important Jewish prayer, proclaiming the oneness of God.

Around two hundred years ago, Rabbi Nachman of Bratzlav summed up much of this in the following prayer, which goes to the heart of Jewish thought and action. Quakers might find themselves at least to some extent in sympathy with it:

*May the will come from You*
*To annul wars and the shedding of blood from the universe,*
*And to extend a peace, great and wondrous, in the*
*universe.*
*Nor again shall one people raise the sword against another*
*And they shall learn war no more.*
*But let all the residents of earth recognise and know the*
*innermost truth:*
*That we are not come into this world for quarrel and*
*division,*
*Nor for hate and jealousy, contrariness and bloodshed;*
*But we are come into this world You to recognise and know,*
*May You be blessed forever.*

*And let your children tell their children, and their children another generation.* Thus begins the book of Joel telling us the eternal truth that we all recognise: that somehow we want to pass on to the next generation the values we have held to be of importance in our own lives. These values have been shaped by both inheritance and experience. The family may be one community where they are shared and re-created; another is surely the school.

There are only a few Quaker schools in England and Ireland, seven in England and two in Ireland. They are flourishing paradoxes. The influence on young people who pass through them is incalculable. What I have to keep at the forefront of my mind each day as I try to fulfil my responsibilities as Head of such a school is the justifiable question: Can you have a Quaker school with so few Quaker pupils and staff?

Their beginnings are various, their histories shorter or longer, though they were once full of Quaker children. Some of the schools have completed their time and exist no more, except in the memory and experience of those who attended or worked in them and have taken their values out into the world.

Well, the values of Quakerism continue to lie at the heart of these schools, accepted and shared by pupils and staff of so many different faiths, all drawn together as equals before God in the silence of worship. The sense of community in the Quaker schools is tangible: in the openness of relationships between pupils and staff, and in the trust and integrity that characterises their daily contact. These are schools where nonviolence is a reality, where genuine and conscious attempts are made to achieve peaceful conflict resolution and where restorative justice can often be seen in the way problems are handled.

As a school inspector and in the course of my work as a Head, I visit many schools, often excellent ones with notable qualities and a distinctive ethos. While certain values are now, or at least should be, common to all good schools, I have yet to find schools that are as genuinely inclusive as Quaker schools, embracing all those of different backgrounds, religions, languages, cultures, and races on a basis of complete equality.

The lack of formal liturgy in worship, but also the strong sense of a community based on spiritual values, enable those of contrasting faiths and of none to feel that their insights are truly valued. No-one feels excluded or marginalised or patronised. On the contrary, the ethos enables views to be heard with sympathy and understanding. The schools reflect and embody, to quote a phrase from the Chief Rabbi that has become a watchword for our time, the dignity of difference.

As a Jew, I am only too aware of how exclusion of one group by a majority culture can lead to catastrophe. In the year which marked the sixtieth anniversary of the liberation of Auschwitz, we have all had good reason to ponder upon the potential of man's inhumanity to man, and to reflect on a century in which the human race sank to unimaginable depths of barbaric cruelty. In the two generations since then, Quakers have as ever, been quietly working behind the scenes to promote peace and nonviolent alternatives to conflict through Quaker House in Belfast, or the Quaker United Nations Office in Geneva, for example. Our joint experience can be such a positive influence for moral good in the world. Where better to attempt to share that than in a school whose education in the fullest sense is based on Quaker values?

Khalil Mahshi, a Palestinian, the then Head of Friends' School in Ramallah, visited Sibford in 1993. My meeting with him was one of the most memorable moments I have experienced as a Head. His visit to England was arranged by Quaker Peace and Service and the World University Service. He had been working tirelessly to promote Palestinian education during troubled times when it appeared as though hope might be reborn, when Yitzchak Rabin and Yasser Arafat symbolically shook hands on the White House lawn. Subsequently however, the yearned for peace was denied.

The Quaker weekly The Friend included this account of my reflection on his visit: *We met on a Monday morning, with a handshake that for both of us had profound significance. Here were two Heads of Quaker Schools from the West Bank and England, one a Palestinian, the other a Jew, coming together with a special understanding and a particular bond that our mutual history has given us. Through our service in Quaker schools, our encounter was made possible. Our shared perception was voiced by Khalil Mahshi after I had experienced the joy of welcoming him to Sibford's Morning Meeting for Worship. As we left the hall, he said quietly: I am at home.*

Whether for Khalil Mahshi or Gerald Priestland or any of the countless others who have encountered Quakerism or Quaker schools, that sense of home has been a reality. It is for me an inestimable privilege to have been able, as a Jew, to experience that home and to contribute a little to it over the years.

These thoughts are a response to an invitation to write on *Quakers and inter-faith enrichment/experience/encounter*. There can be no better conclusion, I feel, than these well-known words of the blessing:

*May the Lord bless us and keep us.*
*May the face of the Lord enlighten us and be gracious to us.*
*May the Lord turn His face towards us, and give us peace.*

**The Author**

John Dunston began his teaching career in Cheltenham, after studying at Cambridge and York universities, and a year in Germany. He was head of modern languages at Bancroft's School, Essex, during the 1980's.

In 1990, John was appointed head of Sibford School, moving to the headship of Leighton Park School in 1996.

John was awarded a Churchill Fellowship in 1990 in order to train children's choirs in China. He has served as Clerk of the Friends Schools Heads' Conference; Chair of the Education Committee of the Council of Christians and Jews; Vice-President of the Oxford Synagogue; and Chairman of the Society of Heads of Independent Schools; and is currently a Reporting Inspector for the Independent Schools Inspectorate.

Interests include: his family, Paris, music, inter-faith relations and the future of the Religious Society of Friends.

# Special Expressions
# A Jewish Childhood

## Eva Tucker

CHARLOTTE'S GRANDPARENTS had a calendar of special expressions for each of the Jewish feast days. Together they thought about God as the different holy days approached. It made Charlotte think about God, too. He looked remarkably like her grandfather. She didn't have to do anything as strenuous as believe in Him. He was just there. The fact that some people, her non-Jewish father divorced from her mother included, didn't think there was Anyone there made no difference at all. Nor did it occur to her for a single moment that He might be She. But Charlotte knew she was only half Jewish. In the Berlin of the late nineteen thirties that was quite a problem.

When the little Japanese vases in the drawing room had snowdrops in them it was time for Purim.

The Jewish Mardi Gras, celebrating Esther and Mordecai's triumph over horrid Hamaan. God was in a happy frame of mind, there were roguish smiles on the grandparents' faces. It was absolutely in order to be a child. The child, das Kind, that's what they called her when they thought she wasn't listening. For Purim the child was allowed to do what she wanted, dress up as an angel in pink crepe paper, for instance. She'd had a dream that she was one of the angels round Jacob's ladder, though she too had to climb the ladder. On the way to the synagogue, wings carefully folded under her winter coat, she was that angel. Dreams do come true. Outside, a crowd of people were shaking their heads at the black swastikas that had been chalked on the synagogue wall. A family with two boys said hallo to them.

"I had no idea the Manns were Jewish" her grandmother said when they were out of earshot.

"Neither did they til quite recently" her grandfather said.

Inside the organ was playing something robust. Charlotte craned her neck to catch a glimpse of the choir in which her great-aunt Fanny sang. She'd promised to wave a handkerchief if she saw her. Purim was not a serious holy day: men, women and children were allowed together downstairs. Charlotte was helped out of her coat by two or three eager fat ladies. She hated strangers touching her so her expression did not match her wings. But almost immediately she was in the procession waving a paper flag. Round and round they went. The old gentlemen with silvery hair wearing white prayer shawls pulled sweeties out of their pockets, some gave away whole bars of chocolate.

The child will be sick.

But as the synagogue got hotter and hotter, the organ played louder and louder and God got bigger and bigger, the child was feeling quite angelic.

Towards the end of March or beginning of April her father brought willow catkins he had picked on holiday in his Thuringian village. It was time to think about preparing for Passover. The grandparents' expressions radiated confident expectation. Of Charlotte. That she was to ask the mandatory questions – Manu-stanu – which the youngest member of the family had to ask the oldest without hesitations, first in Hebrew, then in German, to show that she had understood it. Not to mention some of those round the table for the Seder for whom Hebrew was Double Dutch. She was rather weighed down by their confidence in her. Not that she found the learning by heart difficult but she was troubled by their apparently forgetting that she was only half Jewish. As far as her father was concerned, the willow branches signified renewal, fertility, never mind Passover or Easter. He would not be at the Seder supper. He had raised his eyebrows and half smiled when she told him they laid an extra place for the Messiah. She knew he thought it was silly.

Everyone was much too keen to get down to the matzo balls for her grandfather to take them through the whole of the Haggadah, though when it came to eating hard-boiled egg with salt water which represented the tears of the Children of Israel as they were being driven out of Egypt, an uncanny hush settled over everyone. How much longer...how much longer before we...we too...will be driven from the land of our birth? Some of them were thinking Vaterland. Charlotte noticed that the Messiah's place stayed empty. When she had finished the recitation her grandfather, who was wearing a little black skull cap over his pink bald patch, patted her on the head and smiled. That was the best bit of the whole evening. After that, as far as she was concerned, the ten plagues could visit Egypt as often as they liked.

The summer months slid by without any major festivals. Charlotte thought about God regularly every night before she went to sleep and her granny stood by her as she said two short prayers, one in Hebrew, one in German. They were both confident that if she did it with proper concentration, by and large blessings would descend on her and if they did not turn out to be the ones she specially wanted, then that was all part of the mysterious way in which God moved, which was not for them to question. If there was a shortfall of blessings, then she had better ask herself truly, honestly, in quiet private moments – You needn't tell anyone, not even me – her granny would say, what it was she was doing that God wasn't quite pleased with. When she told her father about this method of self-examination he was quiet for rather longer than usual. Then he said "Your grandparents are both very, very good people." And after another silence "But I don't always agree with them." Charlotte went on looking up at him, expecting him to tell her how he disagreed with them but he said nothing more. But there was a special expression on his face, a kind of all-knowing benevolence so that for a moment God began to look like her father. Until she remembered that he did not believe in God.

By the time there were red dahlias and a few early mauve asters in the vases, her grandparents faces were radiant with heightened consciousness. Rosh-ha-Shana, the Jewish New Year was coming up. At school Charlotte was making greeting cards with Hebrew lettering and drawings. How she disappointed herself with her drawings! She had such clear images of what she wanted to put on paper, but something important didn't happen for her between her head and her hand. She managed some very shaky shofars, the ram's horns that get blown to signify God's letting Abraham off sacrificing his only son Isaac and arranging for a ram to stick its neck out in the thicket. Some of her classmates managed the whole scene.

On the day her granny worked hard in the kitchen to be ready in time for the evening synagogue service. Charlotte helped lay the table. She was allowed to put the lovely narrow pale green glasses with grapes embossed on them in the right hand corner just above the knives in each place. God helped her not to break any.

Her mother, who didn't join in all family occasions by any means, did show up to see the New Year in, usually at the last minute when they were all ready and dressed in their new outfits. She would ring the front door bell, four sharp little rings, they all had their own signals, and Charlotte's granny would say – Na, endlich – at last – and her grandpa would take his gold watch out of his waistcoat pocket and look at it pointedly. One year her mother dashed in deathly pale, saying "The SS…." but her grandfather silenced her with a firm "Not this evening!"

For Rosh-ha-Shana the synagogue was very full, the women were upstairs. Charlotte concentrated on not fidgeting which was quite hard during the sermon. They had places in the front so she could lean over the railing and look down at all the men and single out her grandpa's shiny tophat among all the others. He was an Elder and allowed to hold one of the Torah scrolls which made her feel proud. She could see he was feeling proud, too. Thinking as he held the scroll: Here

I am, a Jew and a respected German citizen. Thinking: My forebears – horse dealers, merchants, lawyers, doctors and one rabbi, German since the middle of the eighteenth century. Dispelling images of Hitler and echoes of that sacrilegious Heil with – Not this evening. Thinking: Not us, they can't mean us? Thinking: If anyone, then the new ones, from Russia, from Poland, OSTJUDEN. Not that evening.

The special expressions for Yom Kippur – Day of Atonement – were quite unbearable. They made Charlotte want to go and hide in a corner. In fact, as soon as the Rosh-ha-Shana celebration was over, her grandmother's face sank several degrees into grief, the Weltschmerz lines round her grandfather's mouth sharpened. Her mother's gall and/or kidney stones started playing up. Her father hovered outside it all, kind but unable to shift the gloom. No-one was taking any notice of Charlotte, least of all God. His All-Knowing Face had disappeared behind the refuse of remembered sins to be atoned for. Hell was not a concept that entered family life, but the few days between Rosh-ha-Shana and Yom Kippur did feel like a descent into the region of abandoned hope, achieving its nadir on the eve of the day, to open onto sackcloth-and-ashes shorelines of extinguished life on the day itself.

Her grandmother's face was pale greenish-yellow, her grandfather held himself ramrod straight as if he were still in his first world war uniform. Her mother was sick. Charlotte combed her dolls' hair and changed their clothes, an activity she normally disdained. A food-oriented household which usually gathered round the table with zestful expectation embarked on a day's fasting. Her breakfast of boiled egg and crisp roll stuck in Charlotte's throat. Her mother was allowed a cup of weak tea. They all looked at her with alienating pity as if twenty four hours' foodlessness was an immense privilege and at the same time a hardship that only they could endure. Then her grandmother breathed the word Totenseelenfeier – celebration of the souls of the dead. For some reason that word sent a flicker of life darting through Charlotte. If the dead had souls that could be celebrated then they weren't quite dead, were they? She wanted to be reassured on this point but knew better than to ask just then, expressions were dangerously lachrymose.

They were waiting for her father to come and look after her while they spent the day in the synagogue atoning. How lucky that there was one member of the family who wasn't Jewish! What did all-Jewish families do with their children on Yom Kippur? The bell rang twice – her father's signal – and she leapt up to open the door, relieved beyond words, words she wouldn't have dared voice, anyway, everything ordinary was so shut down. They greeted her father with ceremonial nods, put on their coats – there had been a row about her mother's who had got herself a cheap looking imitation tweedy thing instead of something dark and expensive. But that seemed forgotten now, her grandmother even put out her hand to brush off some invisible speck to show all was forgiven. In a parenthetical voice she mentioned the food left ready for the two non-fasters. Then she pressed Charlotte's father's hand indicating that she would pray for his sins to be forgiven, too, not to worry about not being Jewish. Charlotte's mother walked straight past him. She had once liked him, hadn't she? He still existed, didn't he? Had he turned into a sin she was going to atone for? What about me? Charlotte thought.

When they had gone she looked at her father, embarrassed in the large flat without the grandparents.

"Where shall we sit?"

They chose the drawing room in honour of the occasion. When her father had settled into one of the green plush armchairs he gave Charlotte the package he'd been holding. She knew it would be a book. It was the latest Dr. Dolittle, the one where he goes to the moon.

"It couldn't be true, could it?"

"Not yet" her father said.

"Read to me!"

"We'll take it in turns"

But before he opened the book, he put an arm round her and told her about a famous naturalist called Charles Darwin who had shown that humans were descended from monkeys.

"Millions of years ago" he added reassuringly. "And when you're older" he went on "you can choose for yourself whether to believe in God or not."

"Can you choose?"

He began to read.

The others came back at sundown with lightened faces.

"I'm famished" her mother said.

The kidney and/or gall stones seemed to have dispersed. She even said a few words to Charlotte's father.

"You'll stay to eat with us?"

But he didn't.

He and Charlotte smiled at each other with their Charles Darwin secret.

There was spiced beef for supper and glasses of lemon tea. Life was pretty well back to normal.

"Chanukah next" Charlotte said.

"Haven't you forgotten Succoth?" her grandfather said.

She blushed. It was true, she'd forgotten about the harvest thanksgiving in the specially erected hut behind the synagogue that smelt of fresh bread and apples and had bunches of blue and green grapes hanging up.

"Have you got your Chanukah present list ready?" her grandmother asked and they all laughed. It was such a relief to hear them laughing.

But before the calendar had reached the cheerful feast of Chanukah, the Nazis had burnt their synagogue down.

*This autobiographical story was originally broadcast on BBC Radio 4.*

*The day the synagogue went up in flames was also Kristallnacht November 1938. It was then that my father thought seriously about the offer English Quaker friends of* his had made at Bad Pyrmont where he went regularly for holidays as a veteran of the First World War during which he had been wounded. Thanks to the generosity of Theodora Clark and her friends Anne Lyall and Ethel Honey my mother and I were able to come to England in February 1939. I was sent to a non-Quaker boarding school Stanmore House in Weston-super-Mare run by their friends May and Winifred Smith where I spent five happy years becoming English. Life was much harder for my mother who started life in England as a domestic servant and later worked in a munitions factory in London. After the end of the war we learned that my grandparents had been deported first to Theresienstadt where my grandfather died, partly of ill health and partly of humiliation that he, a doctor, was infested by lice. My grandmother survived to be gassed at Auschwitz. My non-Jewish father who had stayed in Germany was killed by a British bomb.

I have never been a practising Jew as an adult . Just over twenty-five years ago I began to feel an urgent need for a spiritual roof over my head. I remembered how when I was a child the word <u>Quaker</u> had sounded like <u>angel</u> to me so that's where I took myself. I have been a member of Hampstead Friends' Meeting since 1982. Not long after I joined I found myself taking my own front door key out of my bag as I got close to our Meeting House and I've been going to it ever since. But I don't think I could have got through life without that early grounding my liberal Jewish grandparents gave me. Their steadfastness was all the more admirable in the light of the fact that their own lives were increasingly under threat during the 1930s.

## The Author

Eva Tucker is a writer. Her third novel *Berlin Mosaic* was published by Starhaven in April 2005.

# A Soul for Europe
# Ethics and Spirituality

## Richard Seebohm

GIVING A SOUL to Europe was a brave and constructive idea but the newly appointed European Commission seems to have discarded it.

Jacques Delors began it in 1992. He used the phrase giving a soul to Europe to emphasise that stable relationships between the member states depended on more than economic integration. He set up a Forward Studies Unit (Cellule de Prospective in French). There was a budget line to support non-governmental organisations, associations and federations of European interest – including those with an ethical and spiritual dimension – as part of a Programme for Promotion of Active European Citizenship. Among the Unit's tasks was establishing relations with the faiths and latterly with people of faith and conviction (thus accommodating the humanists). This mainly took the form of twice yearly briefings, though (as the word implies) communication was a bit one way. The Soul initiative was intended to promote values of peace, tolerance and understanding in an increasingly pluralist Europe. With grass roots projects and events such as summer schools in mind, a Soul for Europe committee and secretariat began work in 1993, and from 1994 publicised the initiative and offered opinions to the Commission on the merits of proposals. With the informal agreement of the Parliament, about 50 per cent of the budget was allocated to Soul-related applications.

For some years this all worked, though the Secretariat sometimes found that projects with good faith credentials were not seen as furthering European understanding. The process involved a deeper level of dialogue, visits and discussion than a simple financial appraisal, given that the Committee itself included Catholic, Protestant, Jewish, Muslim and Humanist representation.

Then in 1999, after the dismissal of the Santer Commission, European Union financing procedures were hastily overhauled. The Soul organisation lost its place in the grant awarding system and the idea of earmarking part of a budget became unacceptable. The Forward Studies Unit was replaced by the Group of Policy Advisers. This reported directly to Commission President Prodi instead of to the Secretariat General of the Commission, so the grant appraisal had to move out to an ordinary Directorate-General, that of Arts, Education and Culture. A particularly dedicated official in the Unit was promoted to a different post.

The Soul for Europe Initiative did not lose all its funding. It was obliged to seek autonomous legal form under Belgian law as an international non-profit association. The Committee in October 2003 established its mission as follows:

- serve as a think tank on issues which are related both to dialogue within the initiative and the European integration project
- promote dialogue between communities of faith and conviction and the European institutions
- monitor and support the European institutions in their efforts to foster dialogue among the communities of faith and conviction, and to develop and implement ethical and spiritual values as a basis for an integrated Europe.

But the newly appointed Commission has withdrawn support, and the Initiative closed at the end of February 2005. The Group of Policy Advisers has become a Bureau of European Policy Advisers, with only economic disciplines so far represented. A subordinate 'Group of Societal Policy Advisers' had not, at the time of writing, been appointed.

And yet... The draft constitutional treaty contains in Article I-47 the words: The institutions shall maintain an open, transparent and regular dialogue with representative associations and civil society, but its Article 52 goes on:

1. The Union respects and does not prejudice the status under national law of churches and religious associations or communities in the Member States.
2. The Union equally respects the status under national law of philosophical and non-confessional organisations.
3. Recognising their identity and their specific contribution, the Union shall maintain an open, transparent and regular dialogue with these churches and organisations.

The voice of the Initiative has found expression in symposia or seminars, held in alternate years or more often. Right up to the end, they attracted full support from Commission officials. As just one example, an inter-faith organisation known as the Avicenna Group came up with the concept of founding discord (désaccord fondateur in French). Given that the cultural history of Europe contains memories of wounds, the discords should be confronted and lived with, not renounced and glossed over. They are a powerful tool for dispelling the naïve proposition that the European project is an assault on national and personal identity.

At another event, Grace Davie (of Exeter University) pointed out that we live in a world where people are less likely than before to commit themselves to a specific church, political party or trade union. At least, it is in Europe and particularly Britain that we see this believing but not belonging phenomenon. Elsewhere, faith and identity are more immediately linked. In England especially, we have the luxury, the privilege, of floating along on our past heritage – the church buildings if nothing else. France has her tradition of laïcite, but in private life the lay and the believers coexist as an oil and water mix. Germany has the church tax which helps to keep faith alive in people's minds. The Scandinavians are in the process of detaching their Protestant churches from being cogs in the state's administrative machine.

The EU does not have these relics of the past. It can only be ecumenical. But it still has to reckon with religion. A monk can't be treated as simply an employee of his order. The EU must be ready to respond to new factors such as the higher political profile of Islam. The Belgians speak helpfully of religions as a fait social évident or a social fact of life. Another way of putting that is to say, *The state lives off pre-existing conditions that it cannot itself create.* Thus when it comes to dialogue, the constitution is right to treat the faith people as special, not just another interest group. A set number of adherents should not be a threshold for recognition. There is the social dynamic of churches and faiths competing with each other. In the United States, proselytising, mission, seeking adherents, is a market process, but in the Orthodox parts of Europe it is tantamount to treason. There may be schisms within a church. But freedom of religion and belief is one of the human rights that all the international codes protect.

The European Commission gets lobbied (and indeed wants to consult) whenever it is initiating EU legislation. Sometimes the consultation is structured, for example with aid organisations over World Trade Organisation matters. As the range of consultations increases, the Commission always hopes that the interest groups of a particular kind will speak with a single voice. This is not easy for the faiths. There is no consensus over bioethics. At the Convention drafting the constitutional treaty, Keith Jenkins (then of the Brussels Ecumenical Centre) was given 15 minutes to speak for all the people of faith and conviction including humanists. This was a tall order, given that one issue was whether or not the Treaty's preamble should include a reference to God.

There is also the point that Members of the European Parliament are supposed to express the interests of all those they represent. Single interest pressure groups inhabit a different world to that. Political parties may resent single issue manifestations. We should try to stop the media getting away with saying that any message emanating from faith is really a missionary exercise, proselytising. But if everything is ecumenical, important prophetic messages may be lost. At a time when human rights are uppermost in people's minds, leading to a dependency or claims culture, the churches carry an important social message. By committing oneself to a church, one demonstrates an acceptance of responsibility too.

At another symposium, an Austrian school teacher described how she coped with an influx of refugees from former Yugoslavia, who outnumbered her native pupils. They had a mutually incomprehensible mix of mother tongues. Some who spoke the same language had been brought up to fight each other. Satellite television reinforced their old languages and cultures in their new homes. Her concern was that they should speak German without sounding foreign, in order not to be discriminated against.

At the same event, the head of research at the European Monitoring Centre on Racism and Xenophobia spoke of the two concepts of education that the English language doesn't separate. She spoke in Greek, but in French they are éducation and formation, in German, Ausbildung and Bildung. One is about mere learning and the other about building the whole person. If the EU is serious about *active citizenship*, it is surely wrong to discard the concept of *Soul* as if it were a just another economic decision.

**The Author**

Richard Seebohm was the Representative of the Quaker Council for European Affairs based in Brussels and now serves as the Quaker representative on the Churches' East-West European Relations Network, CEWERN.

# Afterword

## Eva Tucker

> .....**Devout souls are everywhere of one religion and when death takes off the mask they will know one another.**

THREE CENTURIES AGO William Penn thought that. Now in the 21st century, with global communications of a kind he could not even have dreamt of, we can surely hope to know one another while we are still alive. That hope was the guiding principle when, inspired by our late friend Margot Tennyson, I began running Hampstead Interfaith Group in 1995. It is that same hope which underlies this anthology of essays by contributors who have held themselves open to experience the spirit of other faiths.

The essays reflect the striving of Quakers for fulfilment in life, including a quality that, metaphorically speaking, involves a degree of vertical take-off from the quotidian. According to William James the essence of religious experiences, the thing by which we finally must judge them, must be that element or quality in them which we can meet nowhere else, a perception of *something there*.

Once that *something there* has been felt in a faith other than one's own it can lead to a breaking down of inner conflict. Inner conflict if it is not dowsed frequently fans the flames of outer conflict. The discovery that it is possible to accommodate the tenets of more than one faith within oneself because those tenets complement each other leads to a breaking down of barriers of prejudice. That is what the pieces in this anthology have attempted to show.